STORMING THE CAPITOL

UNJUSTLY ACCUSED, UNWAVERING IN TRUTH

JENNA RYAN

Published by Freiling Agency, LLC.

P.O. Box 1264
Warrenton, VA 20188

www.FreilingAgency.com

PB ISBN: 978-1-963701-38-8
E-book ISBN: 978-1-963701-39-5

Contents

Introduction

I had no idea that my patriotic journey would lead me into a storm I never could have imagined.

"Our democracy was attacked."
—*Joe Biden*

"A larger effort to subvert the will of the people."
—*Barack Obama*

*"An insurrection, an attempt to overturn a legitimate
election and ... a concerted effort to try to block
the peaceful transfer of power."*
—*Hillary Clinton*

*"An assault on the Capitol, on the Congress,
and on the very idea of America."*
—*Chuck Schumer*

*"I thought I was going to die. I thought I was going
to be killed."*
—*Alexandria Ocasio-Cortez*

*"An attempted coup, an attempted insurrection,
an attempt to subvert a free and fair election."*
—*Anderson Cooper*

Give me a break.

My name is Jenna Ryan, and I'm a proud Texan through and through.

I've built a successful life for myself here in the Dallas-Fort Worth area. I have a thriving real estate career, I'm active in my community, and I love connecting with people – both online and in person. I've always believed in hard work and honest pay, and I'm proud of the reputation I've earned over a lifetime of doing things the right way.

More than anything, I love America. I believe in individual liberty, and I cherish the Constitution – especially the First Amendment. The right to speak your mind freely is the foundation of our American republic. That's why the 2020 election was so unsettling for me. Everywhere I looked online, there were allegations of election fraud. People were talking about a stolen election and a rigged system. And the media just seemed to dismiss these concerns, calling them "conspiracy theories" and labeling anyone who questioned the results as a "right-wing extremist" just for asking questions.

It was like our right to question the government was being attacked. Facebook and Twitter started flagging and removing posts that raised doubts about the election, and it felt like censorship was running rampant. It was a direct assault on the principles I hold dear, and it shook my faith in the very institutions that are supposed to protect our freedoms.

That's why, when a Facebook acquaintance invited me to go to the "Stop the Steal" rally in Washington D.C., I felt compelled to go. He even offered me a seat on his private jet! I'll admit I was a little hesitant at first. I mean, who hops on a plane with a bunch of strangers? But the chance to join other patriots in making our voices heard was too important to pass up.

I envisioned a sea of red, white, and blue – a united front of patriotic Americans demanding transparency and integrity in our elections. We weren't going to change the outcome, but we wanted to make sure our concerns were heard. We wanted to stand up for the America we love. So, with a mix of excitement and a little bit of fear, I boarded that private jet and set off for D.C. I had no idea that this trip would change my life forever.

I had no idea that my patriotic journey would lead me into a storm I never could have imagined.

Little did I know that my life would be turned completely upside down.

The events of January 6 and their aftermath would thrust me into the national spotlight, making me a national scapegoat in one of the most controversial episodes in American history.

What follows is my story – a wild tale of protest, persecution, and perseverance. Through it all, I've learned important lessons about justice, media narratives, and the powerful forces that, in good ways and bad, shape our Republic.

And now, with President Trump's heroic pardon of patriots like me, I'm ready to talk.

1

A Fateful Invitation

This was about speaking the truth and making our voices heard, even if the election was over. Win or lose.

It was January 4, 2021 – a cold and rainy day in my hometown of Dallas, TX.

I remember browsing the internet on my laptop and my phone that morning, reading news about the recent election results between my client calls, when my phone buzzed with a Facebook message. It was from "Jim Harland."

I knew Jim's name through some mutual friends, but we'd never actually met. The message was unexpected, and what it said stopped me in my tracks.

"Want to go to the Stop the Steal rally in D.C. on my private jet?" it read.

At first, I didn't believe it. I had to reread it several times. I wanted to make sure I wasn't imagining things. Was this some kind of elaborate joke? A catfish situation, maybe? Were they going to ask me to pay for it?

My first instinct screamed, "This is too good to be true." After all, how often does someone offer you a ride on a private jet out of the blue? It had never happened to me before.

My skepticism got the better of me, and I launched my own little investigation. I clicked over to Jim's profile and spent a few minutes scrolling through his posts and photos. I wanted to make sure this was all legitimate before I said anything in response.

Sure enough, there were numerous pictures of him in a private plane and countless photos showing him with people having fun at various events all over the country. His profile seemed real, with a long history of posts and friendly interactions. "Well, maybe this is actually legit," I thought, feeling a flutter of excitement in my stomach.

For someone like me, the idea of flying to a Trump rally in Washington, D.C., on a private jet was beyond exhilarating. 2020 had been a really tough year with endless COVID lockdowns and crazy riots – like all Americans, I'd spent months on end forced to stay home, watching the world seemingly fall apart through my phone and computer screens. The real estate market had been decimated, and my work was slower than ever. Along with millions of other Americans, I was worried about money, my community, and the state of our nation. So this felt like more than just an adventure; it felt like a chance to break free from the monotony and frustration that had defined my prior year. Plus, I knew how important this rally was going to be. It wasn't just another political event – it was our chance to stand up for election integrity, to show the government that we were paying attention and wouldn't let them silence our genuine concerns.

This was about speaking the truth and making our voices heard, even if the election was over. Win or lose.

The thought of being part of something so significant made my heart race.

After careful consideration, I messaged Jim back, saying I was interested. But I had one condition – I wanted to bring my friend, Bill. Having a familiar face along would make me feel safer and more comfortable, and Bill was always up for an adventure. This was important to me.

To my surprise and delight, Jim immediately agreed. It was settled – we were going to Washington, D.C.! The reality of what was happening started to sink in: I was about to fly on a private jet to the nation's capital for one of the most important rallies in American history.

A tiny voice in the back of my mind kept whispering, "Should I really be doing this? It's probably not the smartest thing to go on a trip with people I don't know." The voice grew louder as I packed my bag and made arrangements. But I trusted Bill, and he was already on board and thrilled about the photo ops and the chance to create some great content for our social media channels. We spent hours texting back and forth that day, imagining ourselves surrounded by a sea of patriots, all united in our love for America and our determination to fight for a fair election. His enthusiasm was contagious, and it helped quiet those nagging doubts.

Besides, I reasoned, I was street-smart enough to handle myself if things went south. I'd traveled plenty before, and we could always Uber or catch a commercial flight back if we needed to. The fact that Bill would be there with me provided an extra layer of security. We'd look out for each other, just like we always did.

We booked a room online at the Westin Washington D.C. City Center, conveniently, as we found out later, on the same floor as Jim's room. As we made our reservations, everything seemed to be falling into place like pieces of a perfectly arranged puzzle. The hotel was centrally located, the weather forecast looked decent for January, and our excitement continued to build with each passing hour.

When the day of the flight finally arrived, our excitement was electric. We met at the airport in Denton, and I immediately hit it off with Julie, one of the other passengers. She was stunning – like a supermodel – with a personality to match her looks. Her energy was infectious, and we clicked instantly. We spent time taking pictures on the tarmac in front of the plane – pictures that would later go viral for all the wrong reasons, though we had no way of knowing that at the time. Then we met the other passenger, whose name I'll keep private to protect his privacy. Our little group felt complete as we all lined up for another photo, beaming with excitement. This trip was already exceeding my wildest expectations!

The private jet experience was everything I'd imagined and more. We were like kids in a candy store, laughing, taking pictures, and bonding over our shared love for America. Julie was a natural storyteller and kept us entertained with tales of her flying experiences, thanks to her military family background. The conversation flowed effortlessly as we talked about everything – the election, our personal lives, our hopes for the future, and our dreams for our careers and for America. The cabin buzzed with energy as we shared our thoughts and concerns about the direction our country was headed. It was so reassuring to be surrounded by people who truly understood and who shared my passionate belief in the importance of protecting our American way of life. I can hardly describe how eager we were to stand up for our American rights and values.

There was such a powerful sense of camaraderie in that small cabin, a connection that felt almost magical. I couldn't shake the feeling that we were part of something truly special, something historic. "This is going to be a movie one day," I told Bill with absolute conviction. "Who do you want to play you in the movie?" We spent the next hour casting our hypothetical biopic, laughing at the absurdity while secretly believing it might actually happen someday.

The flight itself was smooth and luxurious, nothing like the cramped commercial flights I was used to. As we soared above the clouds, I felt like I was living in a dream. It felt like destiny had brought us together on that plane, and I was certain that this trip would be something we'd remember forever. Little did I know just how prophetic that thought would turn out to be.

When we landed near D.C., a sleek black SUV was waiting to whisk us away. Jim had clearly thought of everything, and his attention to detail and taste for luxury made the whole experience feel even more special. As we drove through the city, the reality of where we were and what we were about to be part of began to sink in.

That night, we all gathered in our hotel rooms, and the party atmosphere was infectious. We shared bottles of wine and took a few shots, laughing until our sides ached and talking late into the night about the rally and our hopes for the next day. The conversation ranged from light-hearted banter to serious discussions about the state of our nation. We were fired up and ready to make our voices heard, united in our belief that we were standing on the right side of history.

As I lay in bed that night, unable to sleep from the excitement, I knew in my heart that this trip was more than just a rally – it was a chance to stand up for everything I believed in, to fight for the soul of America. And I was surrounded by people who felt the same way and shared my passion and determination. We were united in our purpose, and I had never felt so energized and hopeful. The energy in the room was electric, charged with anticipation for what the next day would bring. None of us could have predicted just how much our lives would change in the next 24 hours.

2

Destination: The People's House

At that point, the last thing on my mind was violence or breaking the law. We'd come to D.C. with pure intentions – peacefully exercising our First Amendment rights.

The morning of January 6th dawned bright and cold, but my heart was racing with excitement. This was it – the day we'd make our voices heard!

I'm not a morning person, but the energy of the day had me buzzing. The anticipation had kept me up most of the night, tossing and turning as I imagined the sea of red, white, and blue that would flood the streets of D.C. the next morning. All I could think about was joining that massive crowd of patriots, all standing together to demand election integrity and secure our liberties for future generations.

I spent extra time getting ready that morning, carefully choosing my outfit – layers are always key in the January cold. I picked out my favorite American flag scarf and a warm red jacket that seemed appropriate for the occasion. After checking the weather app one last time, I bundled up even more, knowing we'd be outside for hours in the freezing cold. When I met the others in the lobby, we were all practically vibrating with nervous energy. Everyone was dressed in patriotic colors, and the excitement was contagious as we stepped out onto the streets of D.C.

Before heading to the rally, our little group decided to take advantage of the short time we had in the nation's capital and do a little sightseeing. The early morning light cast long, dramatic shadows as we meandered down Constitution Avenue. We stopped frequently to snap pictures, pointing out historical landmarks and sharing bits of American history we remembered from school. The magnitude of where we were – the very heart of our American republic – wasn't lost on any of us. I know lots of people live and work in D.C., and these sights and sounds are probably pretty commonplace for them. Heck, maybe it all even gets old after a while. But for us Texans, the whole place was surreal. I think we all felt like kids on a field trip. And knowing that we'd take part in a fun Trump rally later that day made the whole thing even more exciting.

But I remember the atmosphere in the city felt tense. It wasn't anything like back home in Texas. Remember, on top of the on-edge atmosphere created by the ongoing COVID-19 pandemic, 2020 was the year of the infamous Black Lives Matter movement. There were signs and symbols of this movement painted all over D.C. – graffiti on the streets and on the sides of buildings and posters on what seemed like every lamppost along our walk through the nation's capital. The "BLM" movement stood against everything my friends and I believed. We long for unity and freedom – not the kind of Marxism that the BLM movement was peddling around at the time. I think all Americans of every color and background deserve every right in the Constitution, no questions asked. But pitting people against each other based on the color of their skin is not helpful, and that's what BLM was about. We wanted nothing to do with BLM.

As we continued our walk, the tension became more palpable. Lots of the stores were boarded up like they were preparing for a hurricane, their windows covered with thick plywood. Was this to protect them against us or against BLM protestors? We meant no harm, but of course, BLM rioters had been looting cities all around the country. I wouldn't blame stores for protecting their merchandise from rioters like them. The few open stores had police officers standing guard outside, their faces stern and unwelcoming. The looks we got from some of the locals and the police made it obvious that our presence wasn't welcome – they seemed to view us with a mixture of suspicion and disdain. It was more than a little unnerving, but the whole scene only strengthened my resolve to stand up for what I believed in. We were American citizens exercising our constitutional rights, and no amount of hostile stares could change that.

Despite the tense atmosphere, we tried to make the best of our morning walk. We stopped to listen to an elderly man who had set up an impromptu radio station on his wagon, playing Trump's speeches while wrapped up in patriotic blankets to keep warm. The familiar voice of our president rang out clear and strong. I began to feel a surge of pride as we stood there on Pennsylvania Avenue, listening to his booming voice echo off the historic buildings around us. The man operating the radio station had driven thousands of miles to be here, and he shared stories of other patriots he'd met along his journey. Other early-morning rally-goers would stop and join us, nodding in agreement at particularly powerful points in the speech, some even singing along to the national anthem and other patriotic songs when they played between segments.

As we continued meandering toward the National Mall, now almost surrounded by fellow rally-goers, the tide continued to turn. The BLM propaganda and angry faces from onlookers and law enforcement gave way to more and more patriotic American smiles and songs. Things were getting exciting! The streets were quickly filling up with an incredible mix of people from all across America – farmers from Iowa, business owners from Florida, teachers from Oklahoma, all united in their love for our country and in defense of our freedoms. We walked by several vendors on the street side, selling patriotic t-shirts and sweaters and gloves and hats (I bought a red, white, and blue beanie that said "45" on the front, and Jim bought me a scarf). We saw YouTube and Instagram personalities interviewing rally-goers, their cameras drawing crowds of enthusiastic supporters eager to share their stories and express their enthusiasm. We heard a few more radio stations broadcasting, each one playing a mix of patriotic music and campaign speeches. People were decked out in patriotic gear, and some even in full-on American colonial-era costumes! I live-streamed a little bit to capture the moment for my followers and my friends and family back home in Texas, trying to share the electric atmosphere with everyone who couldn't be there.

Ever been to a football game? Walked into the stadium surrounded by pumped-up fans wearing jerseys and hats and holding signs? Strolled out after a win, cheering and singing alongside thousands of fellow supporters, all revved up by the victory? That's what this felt like. We were all here to celebrate. Sure, we were discouraged about the election results, but today was about seeing our President and supporting our freedoms. The air was filled with excitement and anticipation - everyone wondering what Trump would say in his speech, sharing their favorite moments from past rallies, and speculating about which other speakers might make appearances. Some people had been to dozens of Trump rallies all over the country! We were eager to hear what the president would say and were excited about the prospect of getting to take photos with faces we'd become familiar with on TV and social media – politicians and personalities who we loved to support. Some people had brought professionally made signs with clever slogans, while others carried handmade posters decorated with glitter and American flags. The creativity and enthusiasm of my fellow patriots were truly inspiring.

Over the prior year, I'd often felt very much alone back in Texas, worried about the direction of our country and, for much of the year, hardly allowed to leave my house. But now I was surrounded by thousands of people who'd come from all over and who believed in the same promise of America. I couldn't imagine a better way to spend this day than standing alongside fellow patriots to stand up for our freedoms.

To be honest, the "stolen election" was, at this point in time, far from my mind. We were all caught up in the festival-like atmosphere and the joy of being surrounded by like-minded people who shared our patriotic values. The morning had become a celebration of patriotism, unity, and hope - exactly what we all needed after the challenging year we'd just been through. Sure, we'd love it if our president could serve another four years in the White House. But the lawsuits were wrapping up, and we expected the election results to be certified that afternoon – it seemed like a done deal.

Anyway, we never made it anywhere close to the stage. We thought we had got an early start, arriving hours before the scheduled speeches, but lots of people were clearly even more enthusiastic than we were to be there. I wouldn't be surprised if some had arrived hours before dawn to secure their spot up front! As we tried to navigate through the growing crowd, we kept getting pushed further and further back. There must have been 5,000 people between us and the front row, all packed together like sardines, waving flags and holding up signs. Even standing on our tiptoes, we could barely make out the stage in the distance – it looked like nothing more than a tiny platform from where we stood. I was more than happy to linger in the back, where I wouldn't be packed in so tight against thousands of other people all trying to push closer to the stage, trying to get a glimpse of the speakers and everything else going on.

We listened to the speeches in the background as we milled around with fellow patriots. I met dozens of amazing people, took photo after photo, and even did some live-streaming. We talked about politics and the election, but we also bonded over other things – especially our freezing-cold fingers and toes! But after a few hours, my practical concerns started to overshadow the excitement. I was getting a bit claustrophobic. Whether I liked it or not, nature called, and I didn't see any bathrooms. I know that concern probably seems trivial given the exciting moment we were living, but it felt very real to me at the time. Plus, we'd already walked about 10,000 steps (according to my Fitbit), and my feet were starting to protest. The cold was seeping through my layers, and I convinced the group to walk back towards the hotel in search of a bathroom and a brief respite from the crowds.

I have to admit, by this time, the thought of a warm hotel room and a hot lunch was far more attractive than anything else this rally had to offer. And, yes, finding a bathroom!

So we set off for the hotel. As we made our way back, we encountered a man who I later learned was Ray Epps. He was animated and passionate, urging people to head down to the Capitol building after the rally. At the time, his words barely registered – I was too focused on finding a restroom and warming up!

On the walk back, we passed many food trucks. Each one was tempting, but I was just too cold. That hotel room would be nice and warm—I'd get there first, then figure out lunch later! I eventually suggested we take a rickshaw back (I offered to pay for it), and Jim, Julie, and the unnamed friend quickly agreed. However, Bill was still caught up in the day's excitement and decided to stay and continue sightseeing.

That rickshaw ride back to the hotel ended up costing me $100, but it might have been the best decision we made that day (though we couldn't have known that at the time). While the massive crowd was descending on the Capitol, we were back in the comfort of the Westin, relaxing in our room. We ordered delicious WaWa sub sandwiches – comfort food at its finest – and opened a bottle of wine. We settled in to watch Fox News, waiting for what we assumed would be the inevitable certification of the election. Despite our disappointment about the election outcome, it felt like a small victory just being away from the growing tension and chaos of the crowds outside. We got to play a part in the day without still being stuck out there in the cold.

At that point, the last thing on my mind was violence or breaking the law. We'd all come to D.C. with pure intentions – to peacefully protest and exercise our First Amendment rights. The Constitution guarantees us the right to peacefully assemble and petition the government for a redress of grievances, and that's exactly what I intended to do. I wasn't carrying any weapons or looking for trouble. I was armed with nothing but my cell phone and my voice. My only goal was to let my elected officials know that I, and countless others all across America, were concerned about our freedoms and the integrity of our elections. Things just didn't add up, and everybody knew it. I wasn't just going to sit around and do nothing.

Looking back, my biggest worries that day were decidedly mundane – practical concerns about finding bathrooms in the massive crowd (seriously, why didn't they have more porta-potties?!), staying warm in the January cold, and making sure we could find decent food. The thought of getting caught up in some kind of riot or violent protest never even crossed my mind. The worst thing I imagined happening was getting stuck in a crowd or maybe losing my phone. And especially now that we were in the hotel room, the idea of even going back out there was crazy. It was going to take hours to warm up – why would we ever go back out? Wasn't the rally over?

Looking back, I realize that a few hours later, things got out of hand. The simple patriotic journey I'd envisioned back in Texas would soon turn into something far different than anything I could have imagined. I had no idea what lay ahead, no inkling of the events that would unfold that day and the way they would forever change my life. Sometimes, I wonder if I would have made different choices if I'd known what was coming, but hindsight has a way of making everything clearer. At the end of the day, I was here in D.C. to voice my support for our American freedoms – that's something I'll never regret doing.

3

Two Minutes and Eight Seconds

*A feeling of unease washed over me,
my instincts finally breaking through the fog
of excitement and group mentality.*

After an hour or so in the hotel room, I was suddenly hit with a whirlwind of emotions. The rally had been exhilarating - the energy of thousands of like-minded patriots coming together, the powerful speeches, the sense of purpose we all shared, and all in our nation's capital. It was like a dream! But watching the certification of the election results on TV felt like a punch to the gut, knocking the wind out of all our collective hopes. It was official: Joe Biden was going to be president. Even though we expected this, it still felt like everything we'd fought for was slipping away.

We were all disappointed, our spirits dampened by the news. But Julie, who I had quickly learned was ever the optimist, suddenly perked up as she pointed to the TV screen. "Hey, look! They're going in there," she said, her eyes sparkling with a mischievous glint. On the screen, we could see hundreds of people entering the Capitol building – some climbing the walls, others walking through the rotunda. The cameras panned across crowds flowing through the halls like water, waving flags and taking photos. It didn't look violent or illegal at that moment – just a lot of people milling about, almost like tourists on an impromptu tour. A bunch of them even appeared to be live-streaming as they walked around, looking at all there was to see.

Had they opened the doors? Had they been invited in? It was hard to tell on TV.

"Let's go down there," Julie urged. Jim quickly agreed, his face lighting up with excitement as he offered to get a car for us. The suggestion hung in the air, electric with possibility.

Part of me - the sensible, cautious, and still a little cold part - just wanted to stay at the hotel, relax, and enjoy the peace and quiet away from the crowds. My feet were still hurting! "No, I just want to stay here, have dinner, and take it easy," I whined, thinking about ordering more room service and tucking into my warm bed. But Julie and Jim were insistent, their enthusiasm infectious. Peer pressure, the lure of another ride in a black car, and maybe a little FOMO got the better of me. The thought of missing out on what seemed like a historic moment was too much to resist. I'd come all the way from Texas, after all.

Against my better judgment and despite the small voice in my head urging caution, I agreed to go.

As we rode towards the Capitol, I had no idea what I was getting myself into. The city streets passed by in a blur as I sat in the comfortable leather seats, still operating under the reasonable assumption that this was just another peaceful protest – that we were simply exercising our First Amendment rights like countless Americans before us. To emphasize this point, I excitedly pointed out the giant mural on Pennsylvania Avenue that quoted the First Amendment. "Congress shall make no law... abridging the freedom of speech... or the right of the people peaceably to assemble, and to petition the government for a redress of grievances," I read aloud, my voice filled with conviction, the words seeming to validate our journey.

When we arrived at the Capitol, the scene was overwhelming and unlike anything I'd ever experienced. Thousands of people were gathered there, a sea of red, white, and blue stretching as far as the eye could see. There was a palpable energy in the air, an electric current of excitement and determination that seemed to connect everyone present. The pathway up the Capitol steps was open, and we walked right up almost on instinct, our feet carrying us forward as if drawn by some invisible force. I started protesting, chanting "USA" at the top of my lungs, and praying – all while live-streaming the experience for my Facebook followers, wanting to share this momentous occasion with the world.

At some point, a man with wild eyes and disheveled hair approached me, his face etched with concern and urgency. He said something that should have stopped me in my tracks, something that in any other circumstance would have sent me running in the opposite direction: "You know, a protester got shot in there." The words hung in the air, heavy with implications I wasn't ready to process. I didn't even know what to think. What he said didn't fully sink in at that moment - it felt surreal, like something from a movie, something that couldn't possibly be happening here, in America, at the Capitol, in broad daylight. The very idea that someone could be shot during what I still believed was a peaceful protest seemed impossible to comprehend.

I remember thinking, with what I now recognize as dangerous bravado, *If they want to shoot me for speaking out, so be it. I'm not going to be silenced.* But all said and done, I'm not sure I even believed him. Why would someone have been shot? This was America, after all - we solve our differences through debate, discussion, and peaceful protest. Not violence. Besides, there were thousands of people here, regular citizens just like me, carrying flags and phones, not weapons. The man's warning felt like something out of a different reality, one that couldn't possibly intersect with the patriotic gathering I thought I was part of.

I tucked this information into the back of my mind as I stood on the Capitol steps alongside so many others, trying to push away the growing sense of unease. I didn't know what to do with the news, but there was really nowhere else for me to go - crowds on all sides surrounded me, caught up in a moment that was quickly spiraling beyond anyone's control. The cold January wind whipped around us as we stood there, and I found myself wondering how things had escalated to this point. Then suddenly, cutting through my thoughts like a knife, I heard someone yell, "Push!"

What did that mean? Push what? Where are we going? I thought this was a peaceful protest. Can't we just stand here, on the steps of our nation's Capitol?

But sure enough, people around me started to push, and we all ended up right outside the Capitol doors.

All around me, people were funneling slowly into the Capitol building, and in that moment, caught up in the collective momentum, it felt like the natural thing to do – to follow the crowd, to be part of this historic moment. The Capitol is the "people's house," after all, I reasoned. I pay taxes, and this building is funded by taxpayer money. We have a right to be here! Every day, hundreds of Americans tour this building, right? The logic seemed so clear and simple in that moment of heightened emotion. And like I said, the pace was slow, and I was one of thousands of people filing in, phones out, and ready to snap photos of the statues, the artwork, and all the things I had only ever seen on TV.

But as we crossed the threshold of the Capitol, I was momentarily stunned by what I saw. The grand interior I'd seen in so many photos and news broadcasts over the years was totally transformed. The majestic marble halls that should have echoed with the footsteps of lawmakers and tourists were instead filled with unsettling chaos. There was a thick haze in the air, which I later learned was from smoke bombs and tear gas, creating an eerie, battlefield-like atmosphere. The pristine floors were littered with debris, and the usual quiet dignity of the building had been replaced by shouts and confusion echoing off the historic walls.

A feeling of unease washed over me, my instincts finally breaking through the fog of excitement and group mentality. The reality of where I was and what was happening hit me like a physical force. *I don't want to be here. I have no business here,* I thought, the reality of the situation finally hitting me. This wasn't a tourist visit or a peaceful protest anymore - this was something else entirely, something that made my stomach turn. I took a few hesitant steps inside, my feet feeling heavy with each movement. I saw a police officer who seemed to be welcoming people in, but even that didn't feel right anymore. The whole scene felt surreal, like a nightmare version of the Capitol I'd always admired. Then, overcome by the sudden realization that something wasn't right, that this wasn't what democracy was supposed to look like, that this beautiful symbol of our republic shouldn't look like a war zone, I turned around and walked back out.

In my mind, I hadn't really *entered* the Capitol. I'd stepped through the doorway and then stepped back out, my feet barely crossing that fateful threshold before my conscience caught up with my actions, and I turned around and left. The marble floor beneath my feet felt almost forbidden, as if I were trespassing in a sacred space that wasn't meant for this kind of entry. Later, I found out that I was inside for a grand total of two minutes and eight seconds - a tiny fraction of time, shorter than most commercial breaks, yet those seconds would have massive consequences that would echo through years of my life.

Two minutes and eight seconds – that's all it took to turn my life upside down, and it's about as fast as I could have possibly turned back around and walked out, given how many people behind me were pushing their way in. But nevertheless, those brief moments would come to define me in ways I never could have imagined, casting a shadow over everything I'd built back at home. Those few ticks of the clock would become a dividing line in my life - everything before those 128 seconds and everything after. The weight of those moments would follow me everywhere, from social media to job interviews, from family gatherings to casual conversations with strangers.

During those fleeting moments inside the Capitol, I saw no violence. I didn't break anything, I didn't hurt anyone, and I had no intention of doing either. I never entered the Senate floor or any offices. The historical paintings and statues that normally drew tourists' admiring gazes were just blurs in my peripheral vision as my mind raced with the sudden realization of where I was. I was just swept up in the momentum of the crowd right beyond the doors, carried along by a wave of well-meaning patriotism and group psychology that, in the thick of the moment, I didn't fully understand. The crowd's energy, the day's heightened emotions, and the sense of being part of something bigger than myself had clouded my judgment. I didn't realize the potential consequences of my actions yet, too caught up in the moment to see that I was crossing a line that could never be uncrossed for better or worse. Looking back now, those two minutes and eight seconds feel both like an eternity and like the blink of an eye - a momentary lapse in judgment that would become the focal point of countless discussions, legal proceedings, and personal reflections.

4

The Broken Window

As I stood on the Capitol terrace, taking in the surreal scene around me, the full scope of what was unfolding began to sink in.

I finally squeezed my way back outside, pushing through the dense crowd of people still streaming in. Once back out in the cold air, I felt a strange mix of relief and exhilaration washing over me. My heart was pounding in my chest, and my hands were trembling - not from the winter chill but from the sheer intensity of what had just transpired. I'd been inside the Capitol – the "People's House" – and I'd made my voice heard. Now I was out of that mayhem, but the adrenaline was still pumping through my veins, my heart racing with the magnitude of what had just happened. Standing there on those historic steps, catching my breath, I felt like I was living through a pivotal moment in American history. At that moment, I truly believed I was part of something historic, something important, something that would change the course of American history forever.

As I stood on the Capitol terrace, taking in the surreal scene around me, the full scope of what was unfolding began to sink in. The crowd stretched as far as I could see, a sea of red, white, and blue flags waving in the bitter January wind. That's when I noticed a broken window on the front of the building - a jarring sight that seemed completely out of place on this majestic structure. It was a stark reminder that things had gotten out of control that the situation was far more serious than I'd realized. The shattered glass, the curtains billowing in the January wind, the glimpse of an office inside with a child's drawing on the wall – it all felt profoundly unsettling. My stomach churned as

I realized this wasn't just another protest anymore. The peaceful demonstration I thought I was participating in had clearly crossed a line I never imagined we would cross, and standing there, watching those curtains dance in the wind through that broken window, I felt a growing sense of unease about what this day would mean for our country.

A strange thought flitted through my mind as I stood there, watching history unfold: *Should I take a picture?* I didn't break the window, I reasoned, and just observing it wasn't a crime. The journalist in me, the part that had always sought to document and share important moments, was wrestling with the gravity of the situation. Plus, I'd come to D.C. to document this event and share my experience with my followers who couldn't be here themselves. In my mind, I was just being a citizen journalist, recording history as it unfolded before my eyes. I felt a responsibility to capture this moment, to show people what was really happening here, even as part of me wondered if I should just walk away and pretend I'd never seen any of it.

So, I took a photo of the broken window. But when I looked at it, something about it felt off – too impersonal, too detached, like it wasn't capturing the full weight of the moment. The image seemed flat, lifeless even, failing to convey the electric atmosphere and historical significance of what was unfolding around me. My social media instincts kicked in, those same instincts that had served me so well in my real estate career, where I'd learned that personal connection was everything. Through years of marketing homes and building my brand, I discovered that people don't just want to see a property – they want to see themselves in it and connect with it on a human level. I knew that a photo with a human element would be more impactful, more meaningful, and more likely to resonate with my audience.

So I asked someone nearby to take a photo of me standing in front of the broken window. It was a spontaneous decision in the heat of the moment - I wanted to document what was happening, to show people the reality of the situation. Looking back, I realize this was my professional mindset taking over, the part of me that had always understood the power of personal presence in storytelling. Just as I would position myself in front of a beautiful home to help potential buyers envision themselves there, I thought my presence in the photo would help others understand what it felt like to be there, to witness this moment in history firsthand.

Back at the hotel, I posted the photo on Twitter, where I had 17,000 followers, with the caption: "Here's a broken window, and if the media doesn't stop lying to us, we're going to come after you next." The words came from a place of deep frustration with how events were being portrayed in the media. I was watching the news coverage unfold in real-time on multiple channels, and the disconnect between what I had personally witnessed and what was being reported was staggering. The peaceful protest I had participated in was being characterized as something entirely different, something dark and sinister. While we had gathered to express our concerns about election integrity, the media was painting us all as violent extremists intent on destroying democracy. The contrast between reality and their reporting was so stark it felt like they were describing events from an alternate universe.

Let me be clear about that tweet - I was speaking about confronting media bias with truth, not about physical violence. I meant we would challenge their false narratives with facts, evidence, and firsthand accounts of what really happened. But in the charged atmosphere of that day, words were easily misconstrued. The media, predictably, took my statement completely out of context, twisting it to fit their predetermined narrative about what happened that day. They seized upon my choice of words, interpreting them in the most inflammatory way possible, and used them to paint me as some kind of violent extremist. They ignored the peaceful nature of my protest, my history as a law-abiding citizen, and my consistent calls for non-violence throughout the day. Instead, they cherry-picked that single tweet, stripped it of all context, and used it to advance their agenda. Major news networks ran with the story, amplifying this mischaracterization across the country. Nothing could have been further from the truth or my intentions, but in their rush to judgment, they weren't interested in understanding the real meaning behind my words.

I firmly reject violence and destruction of property in any form. I didn't break that window – the very thought of causing damage to our nation's Capitol building is completely antithetical to who I am and what I believe in. My tweet expressed legitimate frustration with media bias, even if the wording could have been better chosen in that heated moment. Like many Americans, I watched in real-time as major news outlets mischaracterized and distorted events. Looking back, I understand how my words could have been interpreted differently, and I wish I had taken more time to consider how others might perceive them. But context matters enormously here. I was expressing the same deep frustration that millions of Americans feel when they see events they personally witnessed or participated in being misrepresented by mainstream media outlets. This wasn't about making threats or trying to intimidate anyone – it was about standing up for truth and demanding that news organizations fulfill their responsibility to report events accurately and fairly, without political bias or agenda-driven narratives.

For better or worse, that photo has become one of the defining images of January 6th, a snapshot that has been reproduced countless times across newspapers, television screens, and social media feeds. I've accepted the fact that I'll always be associated with it, that it has become an inextricable part of my story and legacy. The image represents a pivotal moment when thousands of Americans felt their voices weren't being heard and when frustration with the system reached a boiling point that manifested in ways none of us could have predicted. In many ways, it captures both the passion and the pain of that day – the genuine belief that something wasn't right with our democratic process and the desperate desire to be heard and understood. The image has taken on a life of its own, becoming a symbol that resonates differently with different audiences. Some see it as evidence of wrongdoing, a testament to how things went too far that day. Others view it as a powerful representation of the deep divisions that exist in our country, a visual reminder of the gulf between different American perspectives and experiences. Still, others interpret it as a wake-up call, highlighting the desperate need for real dialogue and understanding between citizens who see the world in fundamentally different ways. What's clear is that this image, like January 6th itself, has become a kind of Rorschach test for our nation's political psyche, revealing as much about those who view it as it does about the moment it was captured.

This experience has taught me profound and lasting lessons about the power of words and actions, especially in these politically charged times. Every photo, every tweet, every casual comment can be weaponized by those with an agenda, twisted and repurposed to serve narratives far removed from their original intent. What seems like an innocent moment of documentation can become ammunition in someone else's battle. Sometimes, it's better to step back, to observe and reflect, rather than rushing to capture and share every moment. The impulse to document everything, while natural in our social media age, can lead us down paths we never intended to travel. These are lessons I've learned the hard way through personal experience and considerable reflection, but they've made me stronger and more determined to stand up for what I believe in. I've come to understand that in today's digital age, context isn't just important - it's everything. And yet, it can be stripped away in an instant, leaving raw content to be molded and shaped by others into whatever serves their purpose. What seems clear and unambiguous at the moment can be twisted into something completely unrecognizable once it enters the endless cycle of media interpretation and social media sharing. The experience has taught me to be more thoughtful and deliberate about how I express myself and to carefully consider how my words might be interpreted by those who don't know me or understand my intentions.

Through this journey, I've also learned the importance of authenticity and staying true to one's principles, even when facing intense public scrutiny. Every word I write, every statement I make, now comes with a deeper understanding of its potential impact and implications. I've learned to pause, to reflect, to consider multiple perspectives before sharing my thoughts with the world. But this heightened awareness hasn't silenced me - if anything, it's made my voice stronger and clearer.

Despite everything that's happened, I absolutely refuse to be silenced or intimidated. Yes, I'm more careful now about how I express myself and more mindful of the potential consequences of my words and actions, but I won't stop speaking up for what I believe in. The mainstream media may have tried to define me by that one moment, that one photo, that one tweet, but I know who I am, and I won't let their narrative overshadow my truth. I'm someone who loves her country deeply and wants to see it heal and grow stronger, someone who believes in the power of honest dialogue and authentic expression. The lessons I've learned about the power of words and images haven't dampened my spirit - they've just made me wiser about how I choose to express my convictions. These experiences have taught me that true strength lies not in speaking louder but in speaking with greater purpose and clarity, always staying true to one's principles while being mindful of how our words and actions might affect others.

5

Suspicions

As I explored the Capitol's grounds, I came across disconcerting scenes that didn't match the overall peaceful atmosphere I experienced.

In retrospect, my experience on January 6th seems riddled with strange coincidences and unsettling inconsistencies—clues that suggest the day's events may have been carefully orchestrated, or at least manipulated, by forces I still cannot fully identify. At the time, I was simply navigating an intense and rapidly unfolding situation. Only later, after seeing who was prosecuted and who was not and reflecting on the odd circumstances that placed me in the Capitol on that particular day, did I begin to suspect that this may have been some kind of set-up.

One of the earliest red flags was my invitation to Washington, D.C. itself. I was contacted on Facebook by a man I'd never met or interacted with before, offering a seat on his private jet to attend the rally. It seemed too good to be true—an opportunity that conveniently placed me in the heart of the action. At the time, I embraced it as a stroke of luck or providence, but now I wonder: Who was he, really? Why me, and why then? Yes, he checked out as a real person who owned a plane, but the timing and the approach felt unusual. It raises the question of whether someone with influence or resources guided me toward a situation where I'd become a useful pawn.

One of the men who traveled with us—someone I met through this last-minute arrangement—was never questioned by the FBI, despite entering the Capitol and going farther inside than I did. This alone is curious, considering the relentless pursuit of even minor participants by federal authorities. Before we took off, he made a cryptic comment: "Make sure you cover your face so you don't get doxxed." At the time, I didn't understand why anyone would worry about being "doxxed" at what was supposed to be a peaceful demonstration. Why the warning? Why did he say that? And why did this man remain untouched by law enforcement? His presence and his immunity from scrutiny unsettle me even now.

As the day wore on, we encountered figures like Ray Epps—a man later identified as an Oath Keepers chapter leader—steering people toward the Capitol, encouraging crowds to move from the Ellipse down to the building itself. His role has since become a hotly debated topic, as he seemed central to directing foot traffic toward the very place where so many would ultimately face arrest and punishment. While other prominent patriots were arrested, tried, and sentenced, Ray Epps escaped with a slap on the wrist. The discrepancy in treatment raises obvious suspicions. If nearly everyone else received harsh consequences, why not him? The selective prosecution suggests that some individuals—possibly undercover agents or informants—were operating on another level.

At the Ellipse, my traveling companion Jim met with a so-called "uncle" and others wearing full military fatigues. Unlike the countless rally-goers dressed in patriotic costumes, these men looked authentic—disciplined, trained, and very much at home in that attire. Who were they, really? Why meet so conspicuously in the crowd? Their presence hinted at an organized structure beneath the day's surface-level chaos.

Meanwhile, I noticed others dressed in military gear or outlandish costumes like that worn by Jacob Chansley, the "QAnon Shaman." Initially, I wondered if these characters were infiltrators—ANTIFA, government plants, or both—adopting conspicuous roles to shift blame onto regular protesters. Only later did I learn that some were legitimate protesters, while others remain unaccounted for. The inability to distinguish real patriots from provocateurs left me uneasy.

As I explored the Capitol's grounds, I came across disconcerting scenes that didn't match the overall peaceful atmosphere I experienced. For instance, a pile of destroyed media equipment appeared out of nowhere. The crowd around me was not smashing things. I never heard anything being broken. Yet, there it was—a heap of high-value cameras and gear, arranged as if to convey a narrative: "Look how violent these Trump supporters are." It felt staged, like a movie prop set up to capture that perfect image of wanton destruction. Who placed it there, and why did no one see how it came to be?

Also, the presence of tanks and peculiar vehicles made the entire scene resemble a carefully crafted stage set. The sudden appearance of these elements, coupled with the lack of immediate arrests on-site, gave the impression of choreographed chaos. If protesters were truly storming a building illegally, why were so many elements in place to make it feel oddly orchestrated?

In the aftermath, the aggressive and relentless prosecution of average protesters contrasted starkly with the lenient treatment or total neglect of certain individuals who were deeply involved. Many ordinary Americans, some guilty of little more than trespassing, found themselves hunted down, arrested, and sentenced as if they were dangerous terrorists. Yet certain figures, present in the crowd and often pushing people toward incriminating acts, evaded scrutiny. The disparity suggests that either these individuals were working with the authorities or that those in power found it useful to let them roam free, fueling a narrative that justified political crackdowns.

I am not claiming to have all the answers. I know I can't name every player or prove beyond doubt that January 6th was staged. However, the sheer number of oddities—suspicious invitations, cryptic warnings, inconsistencies in prosecution, and the presence of strange characters—plants seeds of doubt that are hard to ignore. Many participants like myself walked into what we believed was a legitimate protest, only to find ourselves labeled traitors and insurrectionists.

Over time, as more video footage surfaces and more independent journalists piece together the puzzle, the sense grows that January 6th was more complex than the simplistic narrative told by mainstream media. Perhaps elements within the government or other groups sought to use the day's events as a vehicle for political theatre, a means to demonize certain viewpoints, and a tool to justify unprecedented crackdowns on dissent.

In any case, the suspicion lingers. I will always wonder how I ended up at the Capitol that day, standing next to people who would never face justice, while I and many others became convenient scape-goats. Something about January 6th does not add up, and I believe history will eventually reveal the truth behind this carefully orchestrated drama.

6

The Real Story vs. The Media Narrative

I entered the Capitol building for a total of two minutes and eight seconds. That's it – confirmed by video and admitted by the Department of Justice.

The hours and days following January 6th were a blur of confusion and disbelief. What I had experienced firsthand – a chaotic but ultimately peaceful protest – seemed utterly disconnected from the media's portrayal of the events. The contrast was so stark, so jarring, that I often found myself questioning my own memories. Had I somehow missed something crucial? Were my recollections somehow faulty? But no, I knew what I had seen and experienced that day.

The media's version of events felt like a parallel universe, a dark mirror image of reality where everything was twisted and distorted beyond recognition. In their telling, I was cast as a villain, a dangerous insurrectionist hell-bent on overthrowing the government. They painted me as some sort of extremist ringleader when, in reality, I was just one of thousands of concerned citizens who had come to make their voices heard. The disconnect between what I lived through and what was being reported was so vast it felt like I was watching a movie about someone else's life – a fictional character who happened to share my name and face but whose actions and motivations were completely foreign to me.

I need to set the story straight, once and for all. I can't speak for everyone who was in Washington, D.C., that day. But I can speak for myself, and I'll never stand down from telling the truth.

Here's the real story – my story – juxtaposed with the media narrative that took on a life of its own:

MY REALITY

I entered the Capitol building for a total of two minutes and eight seconds. That's it – confirmed by video and admitted by the Department of Justice. It's important to understand just how brief this moment was – less time than it takes to brew a cup of coffee or wait at a stoplight. I found myself inside the Capitol building after standing outside, swept along by the momentum of the cheering and pushy crowds. The surge of people behind me created a flow that was difficult to resist, especially given the charged atmosphere of the moment.

I saw no violence anywhere that day, I didn't participate in any destruction (it wouldn't have even crossed my mind), and I left as soon as I realized the situation was escalating. In fact, throughout my entire time in Washington, I witnessed nothing but passionate, albeit loud, protests. Those 128 seconds were marked by confusion and uncertainty rather than any malicious intent. The reality was far from what would later be portrayed in the media – there was no master plan, no coordinated effort, just a series of moments where the intensity of the situation clouded judgment. I was caught up in a moment that I didn't fully understand, and I made the decision to leave almost as soon as I entered when my conscience caught up with my actions. Looking back, those two minutes and eight seconds changed the course of my life, though, at the time, it felt like just another part of an already surreal day.

MEDIA NARRATIVE

I was portrayed as a "Capitol rioter," a key player in a violent insurrection. My image, often the photo in front of the broken window, was plastered across news outlets worldwide, accompanied by headlines that screamed "Real Estate Agent Storms the Capitol!" and "Texas Realtor Leads Assault on Democracy!" Every major network seemed to run the same footage of me over and over, creating the impression that I was somehow orchestrating the events of that day. The media painted me as a central figure in what they called an attempted coup, ignoring the brevity of my presence and the absence of any violent actions on my part. They scrutinized every aspect of my life, from my business dealings to my social media posts, twisting innocent comments into evidence of radical intentions. Local news stations camped outside my home, and national outlets ran endless segments analyzing my character and motives. I was trying to overthrow the United States government, they said – me, a patriotic real estate agent from Texas armed with nothing but my phone. The absurdity of this narrative would have been laughable if it hadn't been so devastating to my life and reputation. They transformed a brief moment of misguided judgment into a calculated act of sedition, turning me into a symbol of political extremism that bore no resemblance to who I really am.

MY REALITY

I saw a broken window when I left the Capitol building. It was a dramatic scene, as you can probably imagine - shattered glass scattered across the marble floor, people taking photos, and an atmosphere of chaos that I'll never forget. I didn't break it, and I wish nobody had. The destruction of public property goes against everything I believe in as a law-abiding citizen. But in the heat of the moment, caught up in the surreal nature of the day, I took a selfie in front of it (one of the hundreds of photos I took that day documenting various scenes and moments).

Sure, I might have done this differently if I could go back in time. I might still have photographed the window - after all, it was a significant moment in history that deserved documentation - but I wouldn't have posed in front of it. That action was misconstrued by so many people later on used as evidence of something I'm not. The media seized upon that image as proof of malicious intent when really it was just poor judgment in an overwhelming situation. But again, I didn't break the window myself, nor would I ever condone the kind of vandalism that took place that day. I was raised better than that, and my values run deeper than any momentary political passion.

My decision to take a selfie was a momentary lapse in judgment, driven by the surreal nature of the situation and my misguided desire to document what was happening. The atmosphere was electric, almost dreamlike - it felt more like watching a movie than participating in real events. At that moment, I wasn't thinking about how my actions might be interpreted or the consequences they might have. I was simply caught up in documenting an unprecedented moment in American history, albeit in a way that I now realize was inappropriate and insensitive. Looking back, I know the post I made with that photo was in poor taste. The caption was flippant, the pose was unnecessary, and it all painted a picture of someone celebrating destruction rather than what I really was - a citizen caught up in extraordinary circumstances making regrettable choices. But it wasn't evil, and I had caused nobody (or no window) any harm. The whole incident serves as a reminder of how quickly judgment can lapse in charged moments and how a single photo can take on a life of its own in today's digital age.

MEDIA NARRATIVE

I became the face of the Capitol riot, the "Insurrection Barbie," a symbol of white privilege and entitlement run amok. The media latched onto this narrative with a ferocity that was both shocking and relentless, using my blonde hair, real estate career, and Texas background to craft the perfect villain for their story. Every aspect of my appearance and lifestyle was scrutinized and weaponized against me - my success in real estate was reframed as evidence of privilege, my Texas roots were portrayed as proof of extremism, and even my hair color became a point of mockery and derision.

My ill-conceived tweet about the broken window was taken as a direct threat against our very government, further solidifying the image of me as a dangerous extremist. What was a momentary lapse in judgment became, in their telling, evidence of a deep-seated desire to overthrow democracy itself. They dissected every aspect of my life - my social media posts, my business success, even my choice of clothing that day - to paint a picture of someone they claimed represented everything wrong with modern America.

News outlets seized upon my social media presence, my appearance, and my profession to craft a narrative that fit their preconceptions about the type of person who would participate in such an event. They dug through years of my online history, cherry-picking posts and photos that could be twisted to support their predetermined narrative. Even innocuous business networking events were recast as sinister meetings, and casual photos with friends were analyzed for hidden meanings and supposed extremist symbolism.

They transformed me from a successful businesswoman and concerned citizen into a caricature of privilege and radicalization, someone they could use to symbolize an entire movement they wanted to discredit. My educational background, my business acumen, even my charitable work - everything

MY REALITY

I was a good-willed participant in a meaningful protest that went too far. Like many others that day, I believed in the importance of making our voices heard through peaceful demonstrations. I made some questionable decisions, but I never intended to break the law or cause harm. I was caught up in the emotion of the moment, influenced by the crowd mentality and my own misguided sense of patriotic duty. The energy of thousands of passionate Americans around me clouded my judgment, leading me to cross lines I never thought I would. Looking back, I can see how the fervor of the crowd and the intensity of the situation affected my decision-making. My actions weren't ideal, and I take full responsibility for them, but they weren't driven by malice or a desire to overthrow the government. I was simply a citizen who got swept up in an unprecedented moment of civil unrest, making choices in the heat of the moment that I would later come to regret. The narrative that I or others like me were attempting some sort of coup couldn't be further from the truth - we were protesters who, a few of us, lost our way, and not revolutionaries plotting to topple democracy.

MEDIA NARRATIVE

I was lumped in with the most extreme elements of the mob and portrayed as a willing participant in a coup attempt. The nuances of my story, the fact that I turned around and left the Capitol almost immediately, were lost in the sensationalized headlines and the rush to judgment. Every aspect of my life was scrutinized and twisted to fit the narrative of a domestic terrorist despite the reality being far more complex and human.

The media, in its relentless pursuit of a captivating narrative, effectively erased my individual story, replacing it with a caricature that fit their pre-determined narrative. My brief, relatively uneventful foray into the Capitol building was transformed into a symbol of everything wrong with America, with me as the poster child. The nuance, context, and humanity of my experience were stripped away, replaced by a two-dimensional villain that bore little resemblance to who I really am.

The power of the media to shape public perception is undeniable. They can create a reality that bears little resemblance to the truth through selective editing, inflammatory language, and the repetition of a simplified, often misleading narrative. In my case, the media's version of events effectively demonized me, stripping me of my humanity and turning me into a convenient scapegoat for a complex and deeply troubling event. They took snippets of my life - social media posts, business success, physical appearance - and wove them into a narrative that served their purposes while ignoring the full context of who I am as a person.

The experience was a jarring lesson in the dangers of media manipulation. It showed me how quickly a single narrative can take hold, eclipsing all other perspectives and creating a distorted reality that can have real-life consequences. It also highlighted the importance of critical thinking, questioning the information we're presented with, and seeking out diverse voices and perspectives. Most importantly, it taught me about the responsibility we all have to look beyond headlines and sound bites to remember that behind every story is a human being with their own complex truth.

7

The Media Feeding Frenzy

The media coverage was relentless and unforgiving. They portrayed me as a dangerous extremist, a traitor to my country, and a symbol of everything perceived as wrong with America.

As the media narrative about January 6th took shape, I found myself ensnared in a relentless whirlwind of attention that was both overwhelming and vicious. My phone wouldn't stop ringing with calls from reporters, producers, and talk show hosts, all eager to secure a piece of the "Capitol rioter" story. Some were aggressive, demanding immediate interviews, while others attempted to sweet-talk me with promises of presenting "my side of the story." However, I quickly realized that their interest lay not in uncovering the truth but in sensationalizing my involvement for higher ratings.

Local news stations established a near-permanent presence outside my house, their cameras fixed on my front door like predators waiting to strike. They monitored my every movement, trailing me to the grocery store, to appointments, and even to church. This constant surveillance created an atmosphere where I felt more like a criminal under investigation than a private citizen despite not being formally charged with any wrongdoing.

THE ONSLAUGHT OF MEDIA AND PUBLIC SCRUTINY

What began as a trickle of local news coverage rapidly escalated into a full-blown media frenzy. My image, particularly the photo in front of the broken window, was plastered across newspapers, websites, and TV screens worldwide. Headlines screamed sensational titles like "Real Estate Agent Storms Capitol!" and "Insurrection Barbie Faces Charges!" International news outlets picked up the story, translating it into dozens of languages and spreading my likeness across continents. I became a global sensation, but not in the way I had ever imagined—or wanted. Each new headline felt like another nail in the coffin of my former life.

The media coverage was relentless, unforgiving, and overwhelmingly negative. They portrayed me as a dangerous extremist, a traitor to my country, and a symbol of everything perceived as wrong with America. News anchors dissected my appearance, career, and personality—nothing was off-limits. They unearthed old financial troubles, scrutinized my social media posts, and amplified every misstep and ill-conceived statement I had ever made. Interviews with former clients, neighbors, and even acquaintances were conducted, all searching for angles to exploit. The portrayal was so distorted that the woman I saw described in these stories was unrecognizable—a caricature of rage and privilege that bore little resemblance to who I truly was.

DEATH THREATS AND HARASSMENT

Within days of January 6th, my phone was inundated with calls and messages from individuals threatening to kill me. The volume was staggering - dozens, then hundreds of threatening messages flooded in daily. Strangers, hiding behind anonymous accounts and burner phone numbers, threatened to burn my house down and harm my family. The messages grew increasingly violent and graphic, with detailed descriptions of how they planned to attack me. Messages like "I hope you get raped, you blond bitch!" became disturbingly common. Some even included photos of weapons or screenshots of my home address, making their threats feel terrifyingly real.

These threats came at all hours and from all over the country, creating a constant stream of terror that made it impossible to find peace. Some were crude and obvious, while others were chillingly specific, describing my daily routines or mentioning personal details they could only know from stalking me online or in person. I reported these threats to the police, showing them screenshots and playing voicemails that made my hands shake, but they advised me not to take them seriously, mentioning that such threats were commonplace and suggested calling back only if I suspected someone was physically stalking me. Their dismissive attitude left me feeling even more vulnerable and alone. Fear took hold Despite their advice and began consuming every aspect of my life. As a single woman living alone, I began sleeping with the lights on, jumping at every unexpected sound, and struggling to get restful sleep. The simplest noises - a car door slamming, footsteps on the sidewalk, or a branch scratching against my window - would send my heart racing. I installed security cameras and altered my daily routines, constantly looking over my shoulder for any sign of danger. I started parking my car in different spots, taking varied routes home, and checking my surroundings obsessively. Yet, the phone continued to ding with more anonymous threats, each notification bringing a fresh wave of panic. The constant state of hypervigilance and terror left me exhausted and isolated, trapped in a nightmare of my own home becoming a place of fear rather than a sanctuary.

SOCIAL MEDIA ATTACKS AND ONLINE MOB

My social media accounts transformed into battlegrounds where trolls and haters unleashed a barrage of vitriol, lies, and public humiliation. Every post I had ever made was scrutinized and twisted, with innocent comments from years past repurposed as evidence of extremist views. Photos with family and friends were dissected and mocked, and business-related posts were flooded with hateful comments. My Instagram photos were plastered across hate forums, with people dissecting everything from my appearance to my choice of vacation spots. LinkedIn connections I'd cultivated over the years began publicly denouncing me, sharing screenshots of our past interactions with disparaging comments. Even casual Facebook posts about cooking or gardening were reframed as coded messages supposedly revealing extremist ideologies. Fake accounts impersonating me proliferated across all platforms, spreading false information and damaging my reputation further. These imposters would post offensive statements purportedly from me, then screenshot these fake posts and disseminate them widely as "proof" of my character. Some even went so far as to create elaborate fake chat logs and email exchanges, fabricating conversations that never happened to paint me in the worst possible light.

The harassment extended to my family and friends, who were targeted simply for being associated with me. Old classmates, former colleagues, and even distant relatives became targets of relentless online abuse. Trolls seemed to work in shifts, ensuring that there was always someone online ready to attack. They coordinated their efforts across multiple platforms, sharing information about my daily activities and encouraging others to join in the harassment. It felt like being trapped in a digital Colosseum, with the world watching as I was torn apart. Even when I deactivated my accounts, the attacks persisted through other channels, with websites and forums dedicated to tracking and harassing me. They created elaborate wikis documenting every aspect of my life, twisting innocent details into sinister narratives. The digital mob reveled in finding new ways to inflict psychological torture, turning social media into a weapon of relentless persecution. They even began targeting anyone who dared to defend me online, ensuring that potential supporters would think twice before speaking up.

CAREER SABOTAGE AND BUSINESS DESTRUCTION

The onslaught extended to my professional life as well. My real estate brokerage, which I had dedicated fifteen years to building, began to crumble before my eyes. What had taken countless hours of hard work, networking, and dedication to establish was dismantled in a matter of weeks. Clients canceled contracts out of fear of being associated with the "Capitol rioter," some even demanding refunds of their deposits. People I had known for years started avoiding me, and long-term business partners ceased returning my calls; their silence speaks volumes about the toxic nature my name had acquired in the industry.

The properties I had listed remained unsold as potential buyers refused to work with me despite my stellar track record and deep knowledge of the local market. Houses that would have sold within days in normal circumstances sat stagnant, their "For Sale" signs becoming painful reminders of my professional demise. My phone, once a constant source of new business inquiries, fell silent except for the barrage of threats. The referrals that had been the lifeblood of my business dried up completely as former clients quietly removed my contact information from their networks.

Colleagues distanced themselves, afraid that any connection to me would tarnish their own reputations. Real estate agents who had once eagerly collaborated with me now declined to show my listings or work on joint ventures. Professional organizations I had been active in for years quietly suggested I step down from leadership positions. Even my own team members began seeking positions elsewhere, their careers threatened by mere association with my name. My livelihood hung by a thread as years of dedicated service unraveled overnight, turning my successful business into a house of cards collapsing in a storm. The financial empire I had built through determination and excellence was being systematically dismantled, not because of any professional failings but because of a single day's events that had been blown wildly out of proportion.

PUBLIC SHAMING AND ISOLATION

People began recognizing me on the street, pointing, whispering, and sometimes taking photos. I noticed people turn away with expressions of disgust, pulling their children closer as if I were somehow dangerous. Even people I had known casually from around town - fellow churchgoers, parents from my kids' school, past clients, regular faces from my morning coffee shop - now averted their eyes or crossed to the other side of the street to avoid me.

I stopped frequenting my favorite restaurants, avoided my usual grocery store, and became increasingly isolated. I started shopping late at night to minimize encounters, ordering takeout instead of dining out, and essentially living like a hermit. Routine errands became anxiety-inducing ordeals - a simple trip to pick up prescriptions could turn into a gauntlet of hostile stares and muttered comments. Even my weekly hair appointments, once a source of relaxation and friendly conversation, became tense affairs as other clients requested to be moved away from my chair. I felt like a pariah ostracized from my own community, marked and branded by my involvement on January 6th.

The life I had built in Texas suddenly felt hostile and unsafe as the comfortable environment I once knew became a place of constant scrutiny and judgment. My neighborhood, where I had lived for years and knew every house and family, transformed into unfamiliar territory. Neighbors who once waved cheerfully now hurried inside when they saw me coming. The local coffee shop where I'd been a regular for years suddenly couldn't find me a table, and the familiar comfort of my community dissolved into a landscape of suspicion and silent condemnation.

FINANCIAL RUIN

The media and online attacks led to severe financial repercussions.

I'll never forget the day PayPal, without any warning or explanation, canceled my account, cutting off my ability to conduct business online. Other financial institutions followed suit, fearing association with the "Capitol rioter." Banks closed my accounts, credit card companies canceled my cards, and insurance companies dropped my coverage. I was financially blacklisted, severely compromising my ability to earn a living. The systematic destruction of my financial life left me struggling to pay basic bills and questioning whether I would ever recover. Simple transactions became complicated as I navigated life without access to normal financial services, forcing me to change my company name and operate under a pseudonym to survive—a constant reminder of the stigma I now carry.

EMOTIONAL AND PSYCHOLOGICAL TOLL

The constant barrage of hate and negativity took a devastating toll on my mental health. I grappled with anxiety, depression, and insomnia, with panic attacks becoming a regular occurrence. The world I had known and the life I had built were shattered, leaving me feeling isolated, alone, and utterly broken. Friends vanished, fearing guilt by association, and family members were harassed, forcing some to distance themselves for their own protection. The profound isolation was compounded by the knowledge that millions of strangers were celebrating my suffering.

The injustice was staggering. While I had made mistakes, I had never intended to harm anyone, never engaged in violence, and had never broken the law before. Yet, I was being punished with a severity that seemed utterly disproportionate to my actions. The punishment extended beyond me, affecting everyone in my life and creating ripples of pain that touched countless innocent people. It felt as though the online mob, spurred on by a biased media, had appointed itself judge, jury, and executioner, condemning me without a trial or due process and without even attempting to understand my side of the story.

THE POWER OF THE MEDIA AND ONLINE MOB

The media's manipulation of my image and story to fit a predetermined narrative, with little regard for the truth, showcased the immense power of the media to shape public opinion, destroy reputations, and inflict real harm. The damage extended beyond my reputation to my sense of self, my faith in journalism, and my belief in the possibility of fair treatment in the court of public opinion. The media's focus on sensationalism over truth turned me into a symbol, stripping away my dignity and reducing the complexity of my human experience to mere soundbites and headlines.

But despite the darkness and isolation, I held onto the hope that the truth would eventually prevail. I recognized that the media's version of events was a distortion, a caricature, and I was determined to fight back, reclaim my story, and demonstrate that I was more than just the "Capitol rioter" they had created. This determination became my anchor, the force that kept me going when everything else seemed lost.

The experience of being canceled was a brutal lesson in the destructive power of online mobs and the dangers of a media landscape prioritizing sensation-alism over truth. It revealed how quickly a person can be dehumanized, turned into a symbol, and stripped of their dignity in the digital age, where reputations built over decades can be destroyed in minutes and where the line between justice and vengeance becomes dangerously blurred.

However, amidst the profound loss and betrayal, I discovered the resilience of the human spirit. I found ways to cope, rebuild, and reclaim my voice, uncovering strengths I never knew I possessed and gaining wisdom through my struggles. I learned the true meaning of forgiveness, the importance of grace, and the power of hope. Emerging from the experience stronger and wiser, I became more determined than ever to fight for justice and speak truth to power. Through it all, I refused to let the media and online mobs break my spirit or silence my voice, becoming living proof that even in our darkest moments, there is always a path forward if we have the courage to keep walking.

8

The FBI Shakedown

It was a stark reminder that I was no longer just a real estate agent from Frisco, Texas. I was now a target, a suspect, in the eyes of the federal government.

5

Even as the media storm raged around me, I held onto a sliver of hope that the legal system would treat me fairly. I had made mistakes, but I truly believed that justice would prevail. Having lived my whole life as a law-abiding citizen, I couldn't imagine the nightmare that was about to unfold, the fear and uncertainty that would grip me for months to come.

The first hint of trouble came on January 17, 2021, just days after returning from Washington, DC. My phone buzzed with a notification - a text from a blogger who had been particularly vicious in her coverage, taunting me with the question, "Are you in jail yet?" My heart skipped a beat, but I tried to dismiss it as just another cruel message. Then, minutes later, my phone rang. It was the FBI. The voice on the other end was cold and authoritative, demanding that I report to the Carrollton Police Station within 30 minutes. The casual tone of the agent made it even more terrifying, as if this was just another routine day for them.

Panic surged through me. My mind raced with questions. *What was happening? What were the charges? Was I really going to be arrested? How could this be happening to me?* With trembling hands, I called my attorney, who became my lifeline in that moment of crisis. He advised me to go to the Federal Courthouse in Plano instead, a small mercy in the face of the looming unknown. At least I wouldn't be paraded through my local police station, where everyone knew me and my real estate business.

The hours leading up to my surrender were a surreal blur, like watching someone else's life through a foggy window. Time seemed to slow to a crawl, each minute stretching into an eternity as the reality of my situation sank deeper into my bones. I remember standing in front of my closet, hands shaking as I tried to choose something appropriate to wear, feeling like I was prepping for a role in a movie I never auditioned for. Should I dress professionally? Casually? What does one wear to surrender to federal authorities? Would they allow me to keep my jewelry, my watch, my wedding ring? I settled on a conservative outfit, then changed my mind three times, each decision feeling more crucial than the last.

The fear was palpable, a knot in my stomach that tightened with each passing minute. As I applied my makeup, I wondered if it would be the last time I'd see my own bathroom for a while. Every mundane task took on new significance - brushing my teeth, combing my hair, even lacing up my shoes. I found myself memorizing the details of my home, touching familiar surfaces as if to imprint their texture in my memory. The morning light streaming through my kitchen window seemed particularly beautiful that day, and I couldn't shake the thought that it might be my last glimpse of it for some time.

As I drove to the courthouse, my hands gripping the steering wheel so tight my knuckles turned white, I spotted an FBI agent parked near my garage, his presence sending chills down my spine. He made no attempt to hide his surveillance, his dark SUV a deliberate reminder of the power they held over me. Another agent's vehicle fell in behind me as I turned onto the main road, following at a careful distance. It was a stark reminder that I was no longer just a real estate agent from Frisco, Texas. I was now a target, a suspect, in the eyes of the federal government. The woman who had spent decades building a respectable life, contributing to her community, and playing by the rules had vanished overnight, replaced by someone deemed dangerous enough to warrant this kind of attention.

At the courthouse, the full weight of the government's power came crashing down on me like a tidal wave. The sterile, fluorescent-lit halls seemed to stretch endlessly as I was led through a maze of security checkpoints, each one stripping away another layer of my dignity. The cold, institutional atmosphere felt suffocating, with every echoing footstep a reminder of my powerlessness. I was fingerprinted, photographed, and questioned by a group of stern-faced FBI agents who treated me like I was America's Most Wanted. Their eyes were cold and judgmental, their voices sharp with barely concealed contempt. They demanded my cell phone password, confiscated my house key, and even threatened to break down my door if I didn't comply. The casual way they discussed potentially destroying my property made me realize how little I meant to them - I wasn't a person anymore, just a case number, another face to be processed through their system.

The degradation continued as they methodically stripped away every vestige of my normal life. My jewelry was cataloged and bagged, and my personal belongings were scrutinized and documented. Each item removed felt like another piece of my identity being erased. I felt utterly powerless, stripped of my dignity and my rights, and reduced to nothing more than a series of forms to be filled out and procedures to be followed. I wanted to explain myself, to tell them my side of the story, to make them understand that I was a real person with a life, a family, a business - but they weren't interested. Their minds were already made up, and their judgment had already passed before I'd even opened my mouth.

The charges they read felt like body blows, each one landing with devastating force: entering and remaining in a restricted building, disorderly conduct, and later, obstruction of justice. Each charge seemed more absurd than the last, a twisted perversion of reality that bore little resemblance to what had actually occurred. Obstruction of justice? For what? For tweeting a photo with my attorney? The surreal nature of it all might have been comical if it weren't so terrifying. I stood there, trying to maintain my composure as they rattled off potential sentences and fines, each one more severe than the last. The federal prosecutors spoke with such casual indifference about years of imprisonment as if they were discussing the weather rather than the potential destruction of someone's life. I kept waiting for someone to realize this was all a massive overreaction, for someone to stand up and say, "This has gone too far." But that moment never came. Instead, I watched helplessly as the machinery of justice ground forward, caring little for truth or proportion in its relentless pursuit of what they called "accountability."

The FBI never wanted to talk to me, to understand my perspective or the context of my actions. They weren't interested in the truth or justice - they had already made up their minds. I was guilty, and they were going to prove it, regardless of the facts. Every attempt I made to explain myself was met with cold stares and dismissive gestures. When I tried to provide documentation showing my peaceful intentions that day, they waved it away without even looking at it. The agents treated me like I was already convicted, their minds closed to any possibility of nuance or context in my case.

After being arraigned, I was released on bond, but the ordeal was far from over. In fact, it was just beginning. The terms of my release felt like shackles designed to restrict not just my movement but my very ability to live a normal life.

The FBI's surveillance became a constant shadow over my life, an oppressive presence that followed me everywhere. I felt like I was living in a panopticon; my every move was watched, and my every conversation was potentially recorded. There was a black van parked across the street from my house, its occupants hidden behind tinted windows, a constant reminder of my new reality. The city even cut down tree branches to give them a clearer view of my front door - a detail so Orwellian it would seem far-fetched in a novel. The message was crystal clear: we are watching you, always.

The surveillance wasn't just physical - it was psychological warfare. Every time I left my house, I noticed different vehicles following at a distance. When I went to the grocery store, there would be agents pretending to shop, their earpieces giving them away. My phone would make strange clicking sounds during calls, and my internet connection would mysteriously slow down or cut out when I tried to communicate with my attorney. Even my neighbors began acting differently, and I couldn't help but wonder if they had been approached by agents asking questions about me. The constant scrutiny created an atmosphere of paranoia that made even the simplest daily tasks feel like walking through a minefield.

One evening, as I went out with a friend, trying to maintain some semblance of normalcy, I noticed the van's lights flashing aggressively. It was like they wanted me to know they were there, watching, waiting for me to make a mistake. The next day, two more charges were added to my case. The timing wasn't coincidental - it felt like a game, a cruel and twisted game in which I was the pawn, and the FBI held all the cards. They were showing me that they could disrupt my life at will, add charges at their discretion, and there was nothing I could do about it.

The FBI shakedown was more than just an investigation - it was a calculated show of force, a message to anyone who dared to question the government's authority. Through my experience, they demonstrated how quickly the tools of law enforcement could be turned against ordinary citizens and how easily fear and intimidation could be used to silence dissent. The methods they used weren't just about gathering evidence - they were about breaking my spirit, about making an example of me to deter others.

The experience left me deeply traumatized and disillusioned. The government I had always trusted, the system I believed would protect the rights of its citizens, had turned against me with frightening efficiency. I felt betrayed, abandoned, and utterly alone in a country I no longer recognized. The weight of the charges, the constant surveillance, the fear of the unknown - it all took a devastating toll on my mental and physical health. My personal life crumbled as relationships strained under the pressure. Friends stopped calling, afraid of being associated with me. Family members struggled to understand what was happening. It was the darkest time of my life, a period when I questioned everything I thought I knew about my country, my values, and myself. The America I had grown up believing in - a land of justice, liberty, and due process - seemed like a distant memory, replaced by something far more sinister and controlling.

9

A Guilty Plea,
But Not a Guilty Conscience

The prosecution's case against me was built like a house of cards, constructed from cherry-picked social media posts and sound bites stripped of their context.

Each morning, I would wake up to the stark reality that my life had been turned upside down by a system I once trusted. The familiar comfort of my daily routine had been replaced by a gnawing anxiety that seemed to follow me everywhere. Even simple tasks like checking my email or answering phone calls became exercises in fear, never knowing if the next message would bring more bad news from my legal team. The prospect of facing trial in Washington D.C., a city where the media had already painted me as a villain, loomed over me like a dark cloud. Every news article and every social media post seemed to further poison the potential jury pool against me.

The odds of receiving a fair trial seemed impossibly slim. The political climate in D.C. was hostile, and the narrative surrounding January 6th had become so polarized that finding impartial jurors felt like searching for needles in a haystack. My attorney, who had decades of experience navigating federal courts, carefully laid out my options. His voice carried the weight of someone who had seen countless cases like mine who understood the harsh realities of the federal justice system. His recommendation to take a plea deal was delivered with the gravity of someone who knew exactly what we were up against. The advice was pragmatic, but it felt like a betrayal of everything I believed in. Each word he spoke felt like another brick in the wall of inevitability that was closing in around me. How could I plead guilty to something that, in my heart of hearts, I knew wasn't a crime? The very thought of standing before a judge and admitting guilt to actions I believed were protected by the Constitution made me physically ill. Yet, with each passing day, the pressure to make this impossible choice grew stronger, threatening to crush what remained of my spirit.

From the moment this ordeal began, I had desperately wanted to tell my story to the FBI. I wanted them to see me as a person, not just another case number. I wanted to explain the context of that day to help them understand what had driven me to join the protest. My attorney made multiple attempts to arrange a proffer, reaching out time and time again to give them the opportunity to hear my side. But each time, we were met with cold silence or outright rejection. It became painfully clear that they weren't interested in the truth - they had already written their narrative, with me cast as one of the villains.

The prosecution's case against me was built like a house of cards, constructed from cherry-picked social media posts and sound bites stripped of their context. They combed through my online presence, selecting only the most inflammatory moments to paint their picture. They ignored the countless posts where I had advocated for peaceful protest, dismissed the evidence of my law-abiding past, and overlooked the reality of who I really was. Instead of conducting a thorough investigation, they crafted a narrative that would play well in the media - the story of a dangerous radical who threatened democracy itself.

The thought of facing a jury trial filled me with a bone-deep dread that kept me awake at night. I could already envision how the prosecution would present their carefully curated evidence, how they would use my own words against me, twisting them into something unrecognizable. The media had already conducted their own trial in the court of public opinion, and their verdict had been swift and merciless. The constant coverage had left me emotionally exhausted, mentally drained, and desperate for any way to move forward with my life.

After weeks of agonizing deliberation, countless sleepless nights, and long discussions with my attorney, I made the difficult decision to plead guilty. The weight of this choice bore down on me like a physical presence, consuming my thoughts during every waking moment. Each time I considered the alternatives, I felt my stomach twist into knots. It wasn't an admission of wrongdoing - it was a strategic choice, a calculated move to protect myself from the possibility of a much harsher sentence. The justice system had shown its teeth, and I knew that fighting back could mean years behind bars instead of months.

The charge I agreed to - a misdemeanor for parading, picketing, and demonstrating inside the Capitol building - seemed almost trivial compared to the way I had been portrayed in the media. The stark contrast between the actual legal charge and the public narrative was jarring, like looking at two completely different versions of reality. My attorney explained how federal sentencing guidelines worked, laying out the cold calculations of risk versus reward. But accepting it felt like swallowing poison, a necessary evil to survive in a system that seemed determined to make an example of me. Every fiber of my being wanted to fight, to stand up and defend my principles, but the pragmatic reality of our legal system demanded a different approach. It was a bitter pill to swallow, knowing that sometimes justice takes a backseat to survival.

Yet even as I stood before the judge and spoke the words "guilty," I knew in my heart that I had committed no real crime. I had exercised my First Amendment rights, joining thousands of other Americans in a peaceful protest. The reality of my actions was far from the sensationalized version presented by the media: I had walked through an open door past a police officer who made no move to stop me. I spent just over two minutes inside the Capitol - 128 seconds that would change my life forever. When viewed objectively, without the lens of political bias, my actions barely warranted a citation, let alone federal prosecution.

The media's response to my plea deal was predictably cruel. They seized upon it like vultures, declaring it a victory for justice and proof of my guilt. Opinion pieces and news segments dissected my every word and action, always through the most uncharitable lens possible. The mockery and celebration of my "downfall" seemed endless. But through it all, I held onto my truth, refusing to let their distorted narrative become my reality.

The guilty plea represented both an ending and a beginning. It was a way to close the darkest chapter of my life and begin the long process of rebuilding what had been torn down. But it also served as a constant reminder of how quickly the system can turn against an individual, how government power can be wielded like a weapon, and how the modern media landscape thrives on destruction rather than truth.

Looking back now, I can say with absolute certainty that while I pleaded guilty in a court of law, my conscience remains clear. I never betrayed my country - if anything, I loved it too much and cared too deeply about its future. The experience has left its scars, both visible and invisible, but it has also awakened something powerful within me. What was meant to break my spirit has instead forged it into something stronger. I emerged with an unshakeable determination to fight for justice, to challenge those who abuse their power, and to ensure that others don't face the same persecution I endured. The system may have won this battle, but they failed in their ultimate goal - they couldn't silence my voice or crush my spirit.

10

Sentenced: A System Rigged Against Free Speech

The judge's words made it clear: my sentence was not just about me. It was about sending a message, a warning to anyone who dared to dissent, to question the government's narrative.

The sentencing hearing was set for November 4th, 2021, in Washington, D.C. The day arrived with a suffocating weight of anticipation. I had pleaded guilty, hoping for leniency, praying for a chance to put the ordeal behind me. The morning of the hearing, I could barely eat or drink; my stomach twisted in knots. As I entered the courtroom, the gravity of the moment hit me like a physical force. But as the proceedings unfolded, a chilling realization dawned: this was not a quest for justice but a show trial, a public flogging designed to make an example of me and chill free speech across the nation.

The prosecution, led by Karen Rochlin, seemed less interested in the facts of my misdemeanor case than in dissecting my personality and my politics. From the moment she stood up, it was clear this wasn't going to be a typical legal proceeding about the events of January 6th. Instead, she launched into a 43-minute diatribe about my social media posts, my interviews, and my opinions – all carefully curated to paint a picture of a remorseless, unrepentant "insurrectionist." Every tweet, every Facebook post, every casual comment I'd made was dissected and analyzed as if they were evidence of some grand conspiracy. My words and my beliefs were being weaponized against me, twisted into evidence of my supposed criminal intent. The courtroom felt more like a political arena than a hall of justice, with every word I had ever spoken being scrutinized and reframed to fit their narrative. The prosecution's strategy was clear: they weren't just trying to prove what I did; they were trying to prove who I was.

Rochlin repeatedly hammered on my "lack of remorse," arguing that my statements, many protected under the First Amendment, were proof that I deserved a harsh sentence. She meticulously combed through my social media history, cherry-picking posts and comments that could be used against me while deliberately ignoring anything that showed my true character or peaceful intentions. She pointed to a tweet where I had expressed frustration with Mitch McConnell, highlighting it as an example of my disrespect for authority. She dredged up old posts from months before January 6th, presenting them as evidence of premeditation. She even misrepresented a statement I made on the *Today Show* to paint me as a liar, claiming I had denied handing over my devices to the FBI, even though I had provided them with my house key. The prosecution even went so far as to criticize my public statements about the legal process itself, suggesting that my exercise of free speech rights somehow proved I was unrepentant. Her distortions were blatant, her agenda transparent: to punish me not for my actions but for my speech, my beliefs, and my audacity to defend myself publicly. The prosecution's presentation felt less like a legal argument and more like character assassination, a calculated attempt to destroy not just my freedom but my entire reputation.

The judge, Christopher Cooper, while acknowledging that I had played a minimal role in the events of January 6th and had witnessed no violence, seemed swayed by the prosecution's narrative and the media circus surrounding the case. His demeanor throughout the proceedings suggested he had already made up his mind before hearing my side. The way he leaned forward during the prosecution's arguments, nodding along with their characterizations of me while barely maintaining eye contact during my defense, spoke volumes about his predisposition. His questions, when they came, felt less like genuine inquiry and more like carefully crafted gotchas, designed to reinforce the narrative that had already been established in the media. Before handing down his sentence, he made a chilling statement: "But for whatever reason, your case has generated a fair amount of public interest, and as a result, people will be interested to know what sentence you get, and that sentence will tell them something about how the courts and about how our country responded to what happened on January 6th. And I think that the sentence should tell them that we take it seriously." The words hung in the air like a death sentence for my freedom, each syllable another nail in the coffin of justice.

The judge's words made it clear: my sentence was not just about me. It was about sending a message, a warning to anyone who dared to dissent, to question the government's narrative. The media attention and the public pressure had transformed my misdemeanor case into a political litmus test, and I was the sacrificial lamb. The weight of this realization was crushing

- I wasn't just being judged for my actions but being used as a tool to intimidate others into silence. The courtroom that day felt less like a temple of justice and more like a theater, where I was cast in the role of the villain in a carefully orchestrated performance. Every camera flash, every scratching pen of the journalists, every murmur from the gallery seemed to underscore the fact that this wasn't about determining an appropriate punishment for my actions - it was about creating a spectacle, a cautionary tale that would echo through social media and news cycles, warning others to stay in line or face similar consequences. The understanding that my personal freedom was being sacrificed on the altar of political expediency left me feeling hollow, a mere pawn in a much larger game of power and control.

The judge sentenced me to 60 days in federal prison – the harshest sentence given to any misdemeanor defendant in the January 6th cases. As he pronounced the sentence, I felt the air leave my lungs, my knees weakening beneath me. The courtroom seemed to spin as the reality of the situation crashed over me in waves. This wasn't just about two months behind bars; it was about making an example of someone who dared to speak out, who refused to bow to the prevailing narrative. The severity of the sentence, far beyond what similar cases had received, made it crystal clear that this was politically motivated. It was a staggering injustice, a blatant overreach of judicial authority driven by political considerations and the chilling desire to silence dissenting voices. The message couldn't have been clearer: challenge the system, and the system will crush you.

My sentencing was a travesty of justice, a dangerous precedent that threatened the very foundation of free speech in America. The implications reached far beyond my individual case, striking at the heart of our constitutional rights. It sent a chilling message to every American: if you dare to speak out, to challenge the status quo, to express opinions that those in power find inconvenient, you will be punished with the full force of the law. The system, it became painfully clear, was rigged against those who dared to dissent, designed to silence voices of opposition through intimidation and excessive punishment. The arbitrary nature of my sentence revealed the true face of political perse-cution in modern America – where the severity of punishment depends not on the actual offense but on how effectively it can be used to discourage others from speaking up. The courtroom that day wasn't just deciding my fate - it was setting a precedent for how the government would handle political dissent in the future, using the full weight of the justice system to crush those who challenged the official narrative. This wasn't justice being served; it was justice being weaponized against the very freedoms it was meant to protect.

11

Sixty Days in Federal Prison Camp

The days bled into an endless cycle of monotony. There was nothing to do but eat, sleep, and try to maintain some semblance of sanity.

The reality of federal prison was a far cry from the sanitized image presented in the brochures.

Bryan, Texas Federal Prison Camp, where I was sent to serve my 60-day sentence, was a stark, dehumanizing environment that stripped away any semblance of comfort or dignity. The concrete walls and steel doors served as constant reminders of my lost freedom, while the harsh fluorescent lights cast an unforgiving glare over everything and everyone. The air itself seemed heavy with desperation and resignation, thick with the collective sighs of women who had lost their connection to the outside world.

From the moment I walked through the doors, I was treated like a dangerous criminal, not a non-violent, first-time offender serving time for a misdemeanor. The intake process was humiliating, invasive, and designed to break you down. I was stripped of my clothing, forced to squat and cough, and handed a scratchy, ill-fitting set of prison garb. Even the silly eyelash extensions I hadn't been able to remove became a source of concern for the guards, adding another layer of anxiety to the already overwhelming situation. The simple dignity of maintaining my appearance was stripped away as I was forced to conform to their rigid standards. The guards seemed to take particular pleasure in reminding us of our powerlessness, their commands sharp and impersonal, their eyes cold and dismissive.

The prison was in the grip of a COVID lockdown, turning what should have been a relatively open prison camp environment into a suffocating confinement. Instead of accessing the gym, the library, or outdoor recreation areas, I was confined to a large recreation room – essentially a bare-bones barracks – for the entirety of my sentence. The brochure's promises of email access and phone calls were empty lies. Communication with the outside world was limited to handwritten letters, painstakingly composed with a single pen and a precious piece of paper. I have no doubt that I never saw letters sent to me on account of how little the guards seemed to care and how difficult they made it to address something to an inmate. My isolation was magnified by the pandemic protocols, which meant even less human contact and more time trapped within the same four walls. The windows, covered with thick metal mesh, offered only the cruelest glimpse of freedom – enough to see the sky but never truly feel its embrace.

The days bled into an endless cycle of monotony. There was nothing to do but eat, sleep, and try to maintain some semblance of sanity. The food, while decent at times, became a source of both comfort and stress. The constant presence of other inmates, many serving time for serious drug offenses, created a tense and unpredictable atmosphere. Their stories and their hardened demeanor served as a constant reminder of the harsh realities of the world I had entered. Every meal was a careful dance of social navigation, trying to avoid conflict while maintaining some sense of self in an environment designed to strip it away. The dining hall became a theater of unspoken rules and hierarchies, where the wrong seat choice or casual glance could spark tension.

And to top it off, I was freezing. We all were. The building was cold, and I think that's on purpose. My comfort was of no concern to the federal government, which was treating me like I was some kind of violent criminal and a dangerous threat to my neighbors.

The emotional toll of incarceration was immense. The isolation, the lack of privacy, the constant surveillance wore me down. I worried about my dogs, my business, my life outside those walls. The injustice of my sentence, the knowledge that I was being punished for my political beliefs, gnawed at my soul. Simple things I had taken for granted - a hot shower, a comfortable bed, the ability to choose when to eat or sleep - became distant luxuries. The nights were the hardest, lying awake listening to the echoes of doors closing and the muffled sounds of other inmates trying to cope with their own confinement. The darkness brought its own kind of torment, filled with the whispered conversations of women sharing their fears, their regrets, and their hopes for redemption.

I tried to find solace in yoga, stretching my body and trying to quiet my mind amidst the chaos. I developed a routine of meditation and exercise, carving out small moments of peace in the midst of the turmoil. I clung to the hope that my sentence would soon be over, that I would be able to return to my life, to rebuild what the media and the justice system had tried to destroy. Each day, I would mark off another square on my mental calendar, counting down the hours until freedom. These small rituals became my anchor, keeping me tethered to my sense of self when everything else threatened to wash it away.

The physical environment itself seemed designed to crush the spirit. The fluorescent lights buzzed incessantly, creating a constant background hum that wormed its way into your consciousness. The industrial-grade cleaning solutions used to sanitize every surface left a chemical smell that never quite dissipated. The thin mattresses on metal bunks offered little comfort, while the communal bathrooms provided no privacy, just another reminder of our reduced status as inmates rather than individuals.

The relationships between inmates were complex and often fraught with tension. While some women formed supportive bonds, others manipulated and schemed, playing power games to assert what little control they could in this controlled environment. I learned to keep my distance while remaining cordial, walking the fine line between isolation and over-involvement. Remember, a lot of these woman, hard though their lives might have been, were here for drug- and weapon-related offenses. I had simply walked into the Capitol, snapped a photo, and walked out. The situation was awkward, and the guards seemed to revel in watching these dynamics play out, totally detached and intervening only when absolutely necessary, their presence a constant reminder of the power structure that governed our lives.

But the experience left an indelible mark, a visceral understanding of the power of the state to control and punish. The 60 days I spent in federal prison were not just a physical confinement but a soul-crushing assault on my freedom, my dignity, and my faith in the American justice system. Every aspect of prison life seemed designed to remind us that we were no longer in control of our own existence - from the regulated wake-up times to the strictly monitored meals, from the limited recreation hours to the constant scrutiny of every movement. The experience fundamentally changed my perspective on justice, freedom, and the true meaning of human dignity. It revealed the stark reality of a system that claims to rehabilitate but seems designed only to punish and degrade.

And all of this because I walked into the Capitol, snapped a photo, and walked right out.

12

Released: Rebuilding a Life in the Shadow of J6

My faith became my anchor in the storm. In my darkest moments, when the weight of public condemnation felt unbearable, I turned to prayer and found strength in God.

I remember the day I was released.

To be honest, there wasn't much fanfare. I had wondered if the media would be outside – CNN, MSNBC, even Fox News – waiting to photograph me in the worst shape I'd ever been. I wondered if mobs of angry people would yell insults at me, accusing me of trying to overthrow our democracy with my phone camera. I wondered if anyone at all would be there to meet me when I was finally ushered outside those cold, steel doors.

But to my relief, the crowds never showed up. A friend took me home, and that was it. I was still on edge, wondering if the FBI was still tracking my every movement. I probably wouldn't have known if they were (or are). But I couldn't let those fears keep me from living my life. I needed all the strength and courage I could muster because the fact is, stepping back into the world after 60 days in federal prison was both liberating and terrifying. The physical confinement was over, but the shadow of January 6th, the label of "insurrectionist," and the relentless media scrutiny would continue to haunt my every step. My life, as I knew it, had been completely upended. My reputation lay in tatters, my business decimated, and many of my friends and family had distanced themselves, unwilling to be associated with the "infamous Jenna Ryan." The weight of public judgment pressed down on me like a physical force.

The process of rebuilding felt like scaling a mountain with no equipment. The constant fear of judgment and the lingering trauma of incarceration made even the most basic daily interactions feel like walking through a minefield. Simple tasks like grocery shopping or getting coffee became anxiety-inducing ordeals, each stranger's glance a potential source of recognition and condemnation. My phone, finally returned by the FBI after my arrest became both a lifeline and a source of dread. Every notification brought the possibility of more harassment, more judgment, and more public shaming.

I quickly learned that the media's appetite for my story seemed insatiable. Despite my desperate attempts to maintain a low profile, journalists continued to dig through my past, analyzing every social media post and every casual comment, searching for new angles to exploit. Local news stations camped outside my house, hoping to catch a glimpse of the "infamous J6 rioter." National outlets like NBC, CNN, People Magazine, and 60 Minutes ran special segments dissecting my personality, bringing in so-called "experts" to psychoanalyze my motivations. I became a recurring character in the national narrative, my story twisted and repackaged for maximum dramatic effect. Late-night comedians like Jimmy Kimmel made me the punchline of their insulting jokes, Hollywood documentaries painted me as a cautionary tale, and online commentators on every corner of the internet dissected my every word and action with cruel precision. Even months after my release, tabloids like TMZ and Perez Hilton continued to run hit pieces, recycling old photos and quotes to keep the controversy alive.

Every public appearance, and every social media post, became fodder for another round of media scrutiny and public mockery.

The negative publicity had gutted my once-thriving real estate business. Former clients disappeared overnight, and potential new ones steered clear, fearing guilt by association. Properties I had listed sat untouched on the market while competing agents whispered warnings to their clients about working with me. The harassment went beyond mere social ostracism - death threats filled my inbox, my real estate signs were regularly vandalized, and my office received countless threatening calls. Anonymous critics flooded my business listings with one-star reviews, making vicious comments about my character rather than my professional services. Local real estate groups quietly removed me from their directories, and former colleagues crossed the street to avoid being seen with me, scared of the cruel media and what even a polite smile in my direction might do to their reputation.

The situation became so untenable that I had no choice but to reinvent myself professionally. I changed my company name and operated under a pseudonym just to have a chance at earning a living. But even then, the stigma followed me like a shadow, with internet sleuths working tirelessly to expose my new business identity and sabotage any chance of recovery.

The emotional devastation was all-encompassing. Depression and anxiety became my constant companions, their dark whispers following me through sleepless nights and empty days. The isolation cut deep - watching longtime friends cross the street to avoid me, seeing former colleagues delete our shared history from social media, and receiving returned Christmas cards marked "return to sender." The community I had spent years building crumbled around me like a house of cards.

Yet somehow, in the depths of this darkness, I found an unexpected spark of resilience. It started as a tiny flame, barely visible among the shadows of despair, but it grew stronger with each passing day. Like a seedling pushing through concrete, my spirit refused to be crushed. Each morning, I would wake up and choose to face another day, drawing strength from the very adversity that was meant to break me. I began to understand that while they could take my freedom, my reputation, and even my livelihood, they couldn't take my spirit unless I let them. This realization became my foundation, a bedrock of inner strength that no court verdict or media narrative could shake. I was determined not only to survive but to find meaning in my suffering and purpose in my pain. The more they tried to diminish me, the more resolved I became to emerge stronger.

My faith became my anchor in the storm. In my darkest moments, when the weight of public condemnation felt unbearable, I turned to prayer and found strength in my relationship with God. The quiet hours of meditation and spiritual reflection became my sanctuary, a place where I could shed the labels others had placed on me and reconnect with my true self. I began to see my trials not just as punishment but as preparation for a greater purpose. Each challenge, each setback, and each moment of despair was slowly transformed into a building block for something greater than myself. A small but loyal group of friends stood by me, their unwavering support a testament to true friendship. Their presence reminded me that I wasn't alone in this fight and that there were still people who saw my heart beyond the headlines. Surprisingly, I also found encouragement from unexpected sources - strangers who had followed my story and seen past the media caricature to recognize the human being beneath. Their letters, messages, and words of support became lifelines, reminding me that even in the midst of a national controversy, human compassion could still break through the barriers of political division.

Recovery wasn't a straight line but a winding path full of setbacks and small victories. I learned to focus on what I could control – my response to adversity, my daily choices, and my commitment to moving forward. Some days, success meant simply getting out of bed and facing the world. On other days, I could see tangible progress in rebuilding my business and reconstructing my life. I began to find my voice again, not as a victim but as an advocate for others who had been silenced and marginalized.

The journey taught me profound lessons about forgiveness – not just of others, but of myself. I learned to release the anger that threatened to poison my soul, to let go of the bitterness that could have hardened my heart. Through this process, I discovered reserves of strength I never knew I possessed, a resilience that had been forged in the crucible of public shame and personal loss.

The entire experience - from January 6th through the arrest, trial, imprisonment, and aftermath - fundamentally transformed my worldview. It stripped away my trust in institutions and exposed the brutal realities of a society increasingly divided by political ideology. I saw firsthand how quickly rights could be eroded, how easily justice could be perverted by political pressure, and how devastating the power of media narrative could be.

But from these harsh lessons emerged a stronger, wiser version of myself. The ordeal awakened in me a fierce determination to fight for truth and justice, not just for myself but for others caught in similar storms. I emerged from this crucible, not just surviving but also transformed – scarred but unbroken, challenged but undefeated. I had become a warrior for truth, armed with hard-won wisdom and an unshakeable determination to use my experience as a force for positive change in America. The path ahead remained uncertain, but I faced it with newfound strength, knowing that no obstacle could break someone who had already been rebuilt from the ground up.

13

Finding Purpose in the Aftermath

*Through the darkness, I found my true
calling – not as a victim, but as an advocate
for justice and truth.*

The ordeal of January 6th, the media firestorm, the arrest, the trial, and the prison sentence could have easily broken me. But in the aftermath of that traumatic experience, I found a new purpose, a reason to keep fighting, a way to transform my pain into something meaningful. Through the darkest moments, I discovered an inner strength I never knew I possessed.

I realized that my story was not just about me. It was about the thousands of others who had been swept up in the January 6 dragnet, many of whom were facing far more serious charges and draconian sentences than I had received. Some faced decades behind bars, their lives effectively over before they even had their day in court. Families were torn apart, careers destroyed, and reputations permanently damaged. I felt a responsibility to speak out on their behalf, to raise awareness about the injustices they were facing, and to use my platform, however tarnished it might be, to amplify their voices.

I began connecting with other January 6 defendants and their families, hearing heartbreaking stories of financial ruin, emotional devastation, and shattered dreams. I share these stories on social media and advocate for their release from pre-trial detention in the deplorable conditions of the D.C. Gulag. The conditions there were shocking – inadequate medical care, restricted access to legal counsel, and isolation that bordered on torture. I joined rallies, spoke at events, and gave interviews, determined to shine a light on the human cost of the government's overreach and the media's relentless demonization of anyone who dared to question the official narrative. With each passing day, more stories emerged of prosecutorial misconduct, evidence tampering, and constitutional violations.

My own experience opened my eyes to the dangers of a politicized justice system that seemed more interested in punishment than in rehabilitation, a system that could be easily weaponized against political opponents and dissenting voices. I witnessed firsthand how prosecutors could manipulate evidence, how judges could show obvious bias, and how the media could influence public opinion before a fair trial was even possible. I felt compelled to speak out against the abuse of power, the erosion of due process, and the chilling effect on free speech that I had witnessed firsthand. The more I learned about similar cases across the country, the more convinced I became that this was a systematic effort to silence political dissent.

I began writing, pouring my thoughts and experiences into a book, determined to share my story in my own words, unfiltered by the media's spin. Late into the night, I documented everything - the fear, the anger, the moments of despair, but also the unexpected kindness and solidarity I found among fellow defendants. I wanted to expose the truth about what happened on January 6th, to challenge the prevailing narrative, and to offer a different perspective, one rooted in personal experience and a deep commitment to the principles of freedom and justice. Each chapter became a testament to both the darkness I had experienced and the light I had found in unexpected places.

Writing was cathartic and empowering. It allowed me to process the trauma I had endured, reclaim my narrative, and find meaning in the midst of chaos. As I wrote, I began to understand that my experience, though painful, had given me a unique platform from which to advocate for change. The words flowed freely, carrying with them the weight of truth and the power of personal testimony.

However, my advocacy extended far beyond the January 6 community. I became an outspoken critic of cancel culture, the social media mob mentality that silences dissenting voices and destroys lives with a click of a button. I saw how easily reputations could be destroyed, careers ended, and lives ruined by anonymous accusations and coordinated harassment campaigns. I spoke out against the dangers of censorship, the importance of due process, and the need to protect the fundamental rights of all Americans, regardless of their political beliefs. This wasn't just about January 6th anymore - it was about preserving the basic principles of justice and fairness that should protect every American citizen.

My journey has not been easy. I have faced ridicule, condemnation, and even death threats for daring to speak my truth. Online trolls have tried to silence me, media outlets have attempted to discredit me, and former friends have abandoned me. But I refuse to be silenced. Each attack only strengthens my resolve;

each criticism confirms the importance of my mission. I believe that my voice, my story, has the power to make a difference, to inspire others to stand up for what they believe in and to fight for a more just and equitable society.

Finding purpose in the aftermath of January 6 has been a long and winding road paved with pain, anger, and disillusionment. There were days when the weight of it all seemed unbearable, and the constant scrutiny and criticism made me want to retreat from the world entirely. But it has also been a journey of profound growth, resilience, and self-discovery. Through the darkness, I found my true calling - not as a victim, but as an advocate for justice and truth. I have emerged from the ordeal stronger, more compassionate, and more determined than ever to use my experience to fight for a better world, a world where freedom of speech is cherished, justice prevails, and the voices of the marginalized are heard and respected. This isn't just about clearing my name anymore - it's about ensuring that what happened to me and countless others never happens again in our country.

14

A Call for Justice,
A Plea for Understanding

I am more than a headline, more than a soundbite, more than a symbol. I am a human being, a woman of faith, a proud Texan, and a patriot who loves her country!

Whether we like it or not, the events of January 6th, 2021, will forever be etched in the annals of American history.

For some, it was a day of chaos and insurrection, a violent assault on the very foundations of our democracy. For others, it was a day of protest, a desperate attempt to make their voices heard in a system they believed had failed them. My own experience that day and the tumultuous journey that followed has given me a unique perspective on the complexities of this pivotal moment, a perspective that transcends the simplistic narratives peddled by the media and the political establishment. The reverberations of that day continue to echo through our nation's consciousness, shaping conversations about democracy, justice, and the very nature of political discourse in America.

Looking back, I see myself as a pawn in a larger game, a symbol manipulated by both sides of the political divide. I was the "Real Estate Agent who took a Private Jet to the Capitol Riots" – a convenient caricature for those seeking to demonize anyone who dared to question the outcome of the 2020 election or the many injustices surrounding it. My words and my actions were scrutinized, dissected, and twisted to fit a predetermined narrative, one that served the interests of those in power. The media circus that ensued was relentless, with every aspect of my life placed under a microscope. Old social media posts were dredged up, business relationships were scrutinized, and even my personal relationships became fodder for public consumption. The weight of this attention was crushing, transforming me overnight from a successful businesswoman into a national symbol of political division.

I made some mistakes, I said things I regret, and I accept responsibility for my actions. But I also believe that I was unfairly targeted, that my sentence was disproportionate to my offense, and that my case was used as an example to silence dissent and chill free speech. The selective prosecution and harsh treatment of the January 6th defendants revealed a troubling pattern of political bias in our justice system. While other forms of political protest were celebrated or ignored, those who participated in the events of January 6th faced unprecedented scrutiny and punishment.

The justice system, which is supposed to be blind, seemed to see me only through the lens of political bias. My right to a fair trial, my right to due process, and my right to free speech were all trampled in the rush to judgment. The media, rather than reporting the facts objectively, fueled the flames of outrage, turning me into a villain, a scapegoat for the sins of a nation grappling with deep divisions and simmering resentment. The presumption of innocence, a cornerstone of our legal system, seemed to vanish in the face of political pressure and public outrage. Every court appearance became a media spectacle, with reporters more interested in crafting headlines than understanding the complexities of my case.

But I refuse to be defined by the events of that day or by the labels that have been thrust upon me.

I am more than a headline, more than a soundbite, more than a symbol. I am a human being, a woman of faith, a proud Texan, and a patriot who loves her country. I believe in the power of redemption. Behind the caricature created by the media lies a real person with hopes, dreams, and a deep commitment to making things right. My faith has been my anchor through these turbulent times, providing strength when I felt weakest and hope when despair threatened to overwhelm me.

My hope for the future is that we can move beyond the anger and division that have poisoned our national discourse. We need to start listening to each other, to understand different perspectives, and to recognize our shared humanity, even when we disagree. We need to hold our leaders accountable, demand transparency from our institutions, and protect the fundamental rights that are the bedrock of our American republic. This requires more than just empty rhetoric or political posturing – it demands genuine effort to bridge the divides that separate us, to find common ground amid our differences, and to work together toward solutions that benefit all Americans. And yes, sometimes it means speaking up in powerful ways when people just aren't listening. While I've admitted to some errors in judgment, I'll never regret standing up for our American freedoms.

But I also believe in forgiveness. I have forgiven those who wronged me, those who judged me harshly, those who turned their backs on me. Forgiveness does not mean condoning their actions; it means releasing the bitterness and anger that can poison the soul. This journey toward forgiveness has been perhaps the most challenging aspect of my experience, requiring me to confront my own prejudices and preconceptions, acknowledge my own role in the events that transpired, and find peace amid the chaos of public condemnation.

I ask for understanding, not just for myself, but for all those who have been impacted by the events of January 6th. There are many sides to this story, many perspectives that have been silenced or ignored. We need to move beyond the simplistic narratives, binary thinking, and politically-motivated victimization. We must engage in a genuine dialogue, one that acknowledges the pain, the anger, and the fear that fuel the divisions in our society and give rise to so much injustice. This requires courage - the courage to speak honestly about our experiences, to listen without judgment, and to seek understanding rather than victory in our political discourse.

My healing process is ongoing. I suspect it will be long and difficult, but it is essential for the future of America. We cannot move forward if we are constantly looking back, reliving the trauma, and perpetuating the cycle of blame and resentment against peaceful patriots on the other side of the aisle. True healing requires acknowledgment of past wrongs, genuine efforts at reconciliation, and a commitment to building a better future together. It means finding ways to address legitimate grievances while respecting our Constitution and the rule of law.

My journey, from a rally for justice on the steps of the Capitol to the confines of a federal prison cell and back again, has been a profound lesson in humility, resilience, and the enduring power of the American spirit. I have emerged from the fire, scarred but not broken, and I am committed to using my experience to advocate for justice, to promote understanding, and to inspire hope for an American future where we can come together as a nation, united by our shared values and our common humanity. This transformation hasn't been easy, but it has been necessary - not just for my healing but for the broader healing our nation desperately needs.

Through sharing my story, I hope to contribute to a more complete understanding of the events of January 6 and their aftermath while working toward the kind of meaningful change that can prevent such division from tearing our country apart again. America is too important – I can't just sit back and keep quiet.